The Sacred History of
Braulio Cantero

by: C.F. Espinoza

FlowerSong Press

ISBN: 978-1-953447-50-0

Published by FlowerSong Press in the United States of America. www.flowersongpress.com

Cover Design by SageLight Design

Set in Adobe Garamond Pro

NOTICE: SCHOOLS AND BUSINESSES

FlowerSong Press offers copies of this book at a quantity discount with bulk purchases for educational, business, or sales promotional use. For information, please email the Publisher at info@flowersongpress.com.

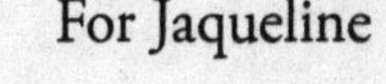

For Jaqueline

It is a solemn thought: dead, the noblest man's meat is inferior to pork.

—Mark Twain

A Hard Living Man

My Abuela's living room is a fucking blood bath horror movie. Or at least you would think so based on how she's yelling at the dentist working on her teeth. The dentist's rubber-gloved hands are jammed into her mouth. The scene reminds me of the internet video where a pot-bellied narco ties a rope around a rival narco's neck. He then inserts a two-foot re-bar between the neck and the rope and twists the rope tight until it rips through the skin, breaks the neck bone, and tears the head off.

My abuela's not being decapitated, but you might think so based on her screams. She is having her teeth worked on, and Monse hates dentists. His smock has no blood, but she's clawing at her cheeks and yelling as the dentist works a molding plate into her mouth. Is my grandmother's living room sterile enough for a dentist to perform dental work?

I'm sure this dentist has performed incisor extractions in kitchens, filled teeth in living rooms, and performed cleanings under backyard porches. I didn't feel pain when he worked on my teeth, an extraction under the desert Mulberry tree in my grandmother's backyard. Still, the flies that swarmed around us did make me pause and wonder about the possibility of infections.

The dentist hunches over Monse. His long legs straddle over Monse's legs. His balding scalp reflects the sunlight coming through the curtains. He whistles as he works on your teeth. Then he pauses, looks up at me, and nods.

When Monse sees me, the pain and tension gathered in the arches of her eyebrows release. She pushes the dentist's hands away from her face and waves me over to hug her. Maybe she's putting on a brave face, or perhaps she's happy to see me. I can't tell either way because she's good at hiding intentions with her warmth. Maybe I'm too stupid to realize that she isn't in pain and only likes to torture the dentist so that he will discount her bill.

She waves me over again, but I can't stomach the sight of a dentist working on an open mouth. I'm not sure how her fear of dentists was passed on to me, but I hate dentists too. Monse is my adopted grandmother, but somehow, I have her very same fears. Every single goddamn one of them. I can't stand the idea of someone working in my mouth. I'm being judged on my tooth decay. *It would help if you stopped smoking. You don't floss enough. You need to brush better.*

My stomach knots and churns at the thought of needing a dentist, and I almost gag.

I nod at my grandmother and smile to hide my nausea before heading down the hallway to my grandpa's room. He is always in good spirits.

My grandpa, Pepper, lies on his bed. He's half-naked, wearing white boxers, no shirt, and one filthy sock. A ring of long silver hairs borders his dark nipples. His skin sags like an old potato, but you can see the outline of his stringy muscles and old bones under that bunched-up skin. His legs are stiff and look like the branches of a pecan tree, brown and ashy.

I tap him on the top of his leathery bald head.

"Ay, cabron," he shouts, then he pats me on the back as I bend over to kiss him on the cheek.

He's watching a boxing match. I recognize the fight, a replay of Duran's no-mas performance. Duran is eating punch after punch.

I dig my tongue into the gap between my molars, feel the rough skin of my bald gums, and try to get the image of Monse and the dentist out of my head, but it won't leave.

Duran waves his gloves up toward the ref and calls it quits. Pepper must've seen me working my tongue into my teeth because he asks if I need to see the dentist. I shake my head no. I sit next to him and watch the end of the match. People are pouring into the ring. They are trying to get at Sugar Ray Leonard.

"Pinche Negro," says Pepper. "Mexicans are the best boxers in the world, and if Duran had been Mexican, he would have never quit."

I lean over, kiss him on his bald head, and listen as he talks about how Mexicans are all heart, but when he talks about how black people are lazy, I leave the room. I stand in the hallway for a second, caught between Pepper's bigotry and Monse's dental work. I decided the kitchen might be the best place to lay low.

I find the dentist washing his tools in the kitchen sink. After rinsing his tools, he dries them with an exaggerated meticulousness, taking his time with the curves and crevices. He shines them and holds them up to the sunlight for inspection.

Monse walks in, working her jaw back and forth like she's taken a couple of jabs to the mouth.

"He's a pinche carnicero," she grumbles.

We don't know many dentists that make house calls, and she swore never to return to a dentist's office after the last guy drilled into her not-so-numb tooth. I can see the dentist's expression change, so I tell her to cool it and thank the dentist for coming to see her.

"You want the dentist to take a look at you?"

I'm back to tonguing that deep gap between my molars. My molars feel like tusks.

I don't want to face that pain. I don't want to deal with that plaque.

"I'm all right," I grunt.

Monse lost most of her teeth at the rate of about three teeth per decade. Every couple of years, she suffered from severe toothaches. She would suck on her teeth and tongue her gums. Sometimes she would wake up in the middle of the night crying out in pain. Aspirin helped, but eventually, she had no choice but to see a dentist. Now she has a nice pair of dentures that look nothing like the fluorescent white plastic dentures she wore in the late nineties.

She lost her dentures recently and called me yesterday to ask if I knew where they were. As a kid, she'd marvel at my ability to find lost things: keys, wallets, glasses, just about anything that was lost I could find. Once, I even found the neighbor girl, Viki, who had been missing all afternoon. Her parents thought someone had kidnapped her. She was in the park sleeping in one of those yellow plastic tube slides in the jungle gym. But now I feel like I'm losing everything. In the last few weeks, I've lost my wallet, keys, and girlfriend, Julieta. Julie and I had dated for six years, but she left me for one of her co-workers, this asshole named Matt.

I couldn't find anything after losing Julie. I even called her one day because I couldn't find my keys.

"Oh, Charlie," she laughed.

Then I heard Matt ask her who she was talking to. I had to hang up the phone before I started to cry.

After that, I knew I needed a limpia, a cleaning of my cosmic sins, a metaphysical reset, and Monse has the bruja touch. Maybe I had exhausted all my karma points, and now it was time to experience some loss. I was getting too deep into my head, falling down that hole of self-doubt and loathing. Hating everybody around and being an asshole to my one friend, Rick. I cussed him out the other day when he asked me for a lighter. Either way, I'd feel better after a limpia. I always do.

As the dentist puts away his tools, Monse collects

the tools she'll need for the limpia. The ritual requires everyday Mexican household items, an egg, palm leaves, a white sheet, a bowl, and holy water. She urges me to sit in the same chair she sat in for her denture fitting. Her baby powder perfume lingers in the chair, reminding me of my youth when she would dry me with a towel after a long bath. I grab onto the memory and don't want to let go. Things seemed easier back then, but that is the thing about memories; we can manipulate them.

Monse looks at the dentist, "You want a limpia, too?"

"Oh no, I don't believe in that."

"You don't believe in God?"

"I should get going." The dentist packs his tools into the sleeve of a leather carrying bag and heads out the door. "Your dentures should arrive within four to six weeks." He opens the door, and the hot desert sun shines through.

I take a seat. Monse stands over me, holding the egg in her palm. She makes the sign of the cross three times over my face. She puts the egg in a bowl and slides the bowl under my seat before throwing a white sheet over me. The beginning of the ritual requires holy water, which she splashes onto the sheet. The cold water sends a shiver up my gut and into my throat. Monse takes my hands and holds them tight. Her hands are warm and soft like crusty bolillo bread fresh from the oven.

I close my eyes and see Julie waking up next to

me. The sun creeps in through the blinds, and I can see the curve of her body beneath the sheets. The day's promise. Julie's hair smells like clove cigarettes. I put my hand on her hips and lightly thrust my hips into her rump. Julie snores a light snore, a little gift only I get to hear. I fall weightless into my memories of Julie. But like all memories of lost lovers, they are horrid and dark. *Did she spend the night with Matt? Does she take deep breaths into his chest after they have sex? Does she smack him on the arm when he passes gas?* I fall deep into this dark well. I remember the time we went to Matt's apartment for a party. I didn't see any signs, or maybe I did, but I didn't want to notice them. They weren't flirting or anything like that. Were they fucking then? I remember how much she held onto my arm that night like we were walking through a haunted house. After a few beers and a shot of tequila, she pulled me into the restroom and asked me to fuck her. I refused because her boss was there, and I didn't want those assholes she worked with to think she was easy or loose.

I'm going deep into this fucking hole. Nothing like living in the past and thinking about your ex sleeping with someone else to twist your heart up. Masochist.

My palms sweat, and heat builds up in my head. So I open my eyes. I can see Monse's outline through the sheet over my face. I can smell the clove cigarettes and Monse's baby powder perfume. My head boils. I can't breathe. I want to run away. I want to jump up and run out of the house. My mouth dries, I can't move, I can't breathe. Heat radiates from Monse's hands. I am cooking alive. I need comfort. I need love. I need to hear the words I love you, Charlie. And that's when I hear Julie's voice, but I can't make out the words.

Monse splashes me with holy water, and I take a long deep breath, but before I can exhale, she smacks me with the palm leaves and utters a few words from the Our Father in an ancestral tone. This guttural sound vibrates in my eardrums, soothing me and tickling my coccyx. I breathe to the cadence of her prayer. We are locked into the same rhythm, a syncopated growl. She splashes more holy water before she smacks me across the face with the palm leaves. I can feel the welts on my cheeks. Smack. Smack. Smack. I yell for her to stop. Instead, she prays louder and swings the palm leaves faster and harder.

The holy water makes the welts on my face burn. I yell again, but Monse is too deep into the prayer. I try to stand up. She pushes me down. The sheet comes off my face. I look into her eyes, but her eyes are rolled up into the back of her head. All I see are the whites of her eyes and the deep red veins rivering through the white. She keeps slapping me with the palm leaves. With every hit, I picture Julie. I can't take it, I need to jump off the chair, but Monse pushes me down again. Monse pushes so hard that the chair slides back. She reaches for the egg in the bowl and uses it to make the sign of the cross over me before putting it back into the bowl.

I try to hold back a small gasp.

Nothing like watching Monse cook, spiritually.

She grabs my head and prays harder like she's

crying. Like she's sobbing. My breathing builds steam again, and I'm almost panting. We both are gulping for air. My thigh muscles twitch. I panic and blackout for a second

Then, my Abuelita lets me go.

Everything is silent.

My heart slows down.

I eye the afternoon sun piercing through the curtains. The luminous world blurred and bleached white by the afternoon sun.

Monse tugs at my shoulders as if to straighten my posture. I sit up. Then a sharp whistle comes from the left, and smack, the palm leaves hit me. Left then right. I try to put my hands up, but I can't move.

"Stop," I yell.

But Monse won't stop. Not until the ritual is over.

She ends the ritual by pouring holy water into her palm and putting her palm over my mouth like she's trying to keep me quiet. My Grandmother pulls the sheet from my lap like she's revealing a magic trick. I see one last flash of Julie's face, it's the face she makes when we make love, but before I can focus on the details of her lips, the image is gone. I try to remember what she looks like, but I can't.

The trance breaks when I hear the crack of the egg's shell. Some of the goo from the egg spills onto the floor. She tilts the bowl to show me the egg yoke. It has streaks of what looks like red blood running through the yolk.

"Sangre," whispers Monse.

I sob fat, shameful, uncontrollable tears.

Monse doesn't say a word.

Instead, Monse walks to the kitchen and pulls a comal and two pans from the stove. I'm sitting in the living room dumbfounded. She opens the fridge and pulls out all kinds of food. Weenies, eggs, and tortillas. She slices a weenie into the pan, then cracks two eggs and mixes it all up. In another pan, she heats beans and grates muenster cheese. The tortillas puff up with steam.

The smell takes me back to my childhood when I'd wake up early to help Monse pack Pepper's lunch for work. The entire house smells delicious.

I pull myself together and wipe the tears from my cheeks before walking over and sitting at the kitchen table. I stare at the bowl with the egg yolk from the limpia. The gooey, bloody yoke reminds me of period blood.

Monse places two burritos in front of me and sits at my side. I'm starving, and my stomach is queasy from this morning's hangover. The bean juice runs down my chin as I bite into the perfectly rolled burrito. Monse licks a napkin and dabs at my chin. The napkin is soaked with Monse's spittle, and I duck and dodge her as she dabs at my face. I push her hand away, but before I can return to eating, she smears the napkin across my face. I pull away, disgusted by her saliva. I get up to wash my face at the kitchen sink and return with some foil to wrap up the burritos.

"Cometelo," Monse nods.

I can't because Monse's saliva has knotted my stomach.

"I have to go," I say. "Don't want to miss the bus."

I ask her if she needs money for her dentures, but she laughs. I can see the gaps in her missing teeth.

"You don't even have a job."

I'm sure my Uncle, Jesus, has told her about my quitting West Texas Telemarketing. He got me the job. I worked under his team, but I couldn't stand that fucking place. Besides, Hey-Zeus always runs his fat fuck mouth. Hey-Zues told the team all kinds of embarrassing shit about me. Like when I was a kid, I pretended to be He-Man and ran around in my underwear waving my baby dick around, calling out to castle Greyskull. "I have the power!" he'd say in the lunchroom whenever I walked in. The worst came when I broke up with Julie. We had worked together for a few months before she found another job as a waitress at one of those chain Italian restaurants. I hated work after she left. When she broke up with me, that asshole Zeus announced our break up to the entire fucking team.

The whole day, greasy ass, grinning, sly gold-chain-wearing fucks asked me if it would be cool if they called her. I was boiling over and almost hit this one guy Jerry. That's why I got canned. In the past, when some fool would crawl out from his shitty cubicle and creep on Julie, Zeus would send his ass packing. After the breakup, it was open season. I had to leave. I couldn't work someplace where motherfuckers would constantly be asking me about Julie. The thought that she would give some slick-haired greasy-fuck co-worker a hand job in the parking lot during lunch break me drove me mad. I had to leave.

Maybe Monse asked me over to chew my ass out for losing a job. Maybe the whole *help me find my teeth* was a ruse. How could I lose a job where my uncle, her son, had been my supervisor. But after a month of fried bologna, ramen soup, microwave pizza, and no Julie, this visit was worth the thick guilt about to be laid down on me by Monse.

I worked in customer service and sales at a call center for Jessica Lyne. This clothing company specializes in plus-size women's attire. I'm talking triple XL clothes for gorditas on the phone. Sometimes they'd breathe all heavy into the phone, and I'd get a little hard because it sounded like a throaty whisper that travels down your thighs and tickles your cookies. Sometimes they flirted, and I would flirt back. I'd get into it, too, especially after smoking a bowl in the parking lot during our mandated fifteen-minute break. That little break kept my mind from crawling through the fucking walls. I would have stayed despite Julie leaving, but between the fucks asking about Julie and Jesus talking shit, I had to go.

One day in the lunchroom, Jesus —or Zeus, which he made everybody call him— told the other employees that when I was a little kid, I would pretend to get sick so that Monse would insert a suppository into my anus. Jesus and some of his lackeys, El Steve, and a guy we all called Spider McGee started calling me Supositorio Boy. This was back when I was still with Julie. She told me to ignore it. But it's hard to mac a chick when your boss slash uncle calls you Supositorio Boy at the end of an add-on sales meeting. He'd say shit like if you look at Supositorio Boy's numbers, you'll see he had a spike in tunics this week.

Between Jesus and these fuckboys, I fucking quit!

Monse's guilt trips always start the same. She tells me how worried she is for me. How she cries at night wondering about her little boy, Charlie. Then she drags some poor memory out from the past. She reminds me of the Bronco swapmeet, where she would buy me little plastic luchadores. The worst of it is she knows how to craft a story. The details, the imagery, it's all there. So when she reminds me about the time it rained, and we had to stop at McDonald's, I can feel the rain and smell the greasy Chicken Nuggets.

Today, she reminds me of when she picked me up from school during the rain and how I ignored her because the other kids laughed at her wet blouse and massive breasts. Then she twists her guilt knife in and reminds me that I owe her three hundred dollars that she lent me to pay my bills and buy Julie some flowers.

Which Julie never thanked me for. Instead, Julie called me to remind me that it was over and that I shouldn't be sending her flowers, especially not to her work. I wanted that fucker, Matt, to see the flowers. I wanted him to hurt. I only ended up breaking and embarrassing myself. Long-stem roses weren't going to fix anything.

I don't want to talk to Monse about that shitty Jessica Lyne job. I try diverting the conversation by telling her I've applied at Azul's. They need cooks, and they pay more than the call center.

"What do you know about cooking," she laughs and points to the burritos in my hand. "That's how you cook," she says.

I let her get out her insults. Which includes calling Julie a whore. When she's done, I stand up, kiss her on the cheek and then head to the front door. As I head out, I see Pepper poke his head from the hallway. He sniffs the air like a mustached Mexican Nosferatu.

"Did you make me some, too, Vieja?" he asks from the shadows of the hallway.

"Sharlie told me you were asleep," she says.

I hand him my burritos and kiss him on the cheek. He refuses and pushes them back into my hand.

He offers me a ride back to my apartment.

Of course, Monse had made him some burritos too, but she likes to give him a hard time. She always has. He takes a burrito and wolfs it down in three bites.

When he's done, he goes to his room to get dressed and find his keys.

It's so hot outside that the soles of my cheap Chuck Taylor knockoffs are melting into the concrete. But I'd rather wait outside than listen to my toothless grandma cackle at my woes.

Eventually, Pepper emerges from the house, his lips glossy from the bean juice. We climb into his '89 F-150 Lariat. He starts it up, then hits play on the tape player. I remember the song from when I was a kid. Pepper tells me he found the cassette in Monse's dresser. The speakers crackle before Ramón Ayala's voice and accordion come on, kick in.

He drives down the border highway, and we sit silently, listening to the tape. We listen till the A-side of the tape ends, and the tape player's mechanisms flip the tape over.

I watch the houses along the border highway and lose myself in the past when the highway, which was just a street, and I first heard Ayala twenty-five years ago. Before the border highway cut off the lower valley farmlands from the Rio Grande River. This entire freeway had once been an access road for the farmers. The water supply was cut off after they built the highway and reinforced the border. What once was a series of long neat rows of cotton and chile stretched across the rust-colored desert arose HUD housing apartments.

I can see a faint outline of the forty-five-foot limestone Jesus Christ statue on Mount Cristo Rey in the distance. This mountain straddles Juarez and El Paso. And Jesus Christ sits on top, his arms stretched out.

My Grandfather and I climbed that mountain every year to meet up with the living members of the Amalgamated Meat Packers Union. Pepper had worked at the Payton Meats factory in central El Paso for twenty-seven years before retiring.

Every year the living members of the AMPU made a pilgrimage up Mt. Cristo Rey on the first Saturday in April in honor of the 61'strike at the Payton meat factory. It is the longest strike in the history of the United States. Can you imagine thousands of grills across America with roaring flames and no weenies, burgers, or steaks to throw on the grill? These were tough times for this great nation. So after four years of strikes, Payton met with the union leaders, and they came to an agreement.

Every April, at the feet of a forty-five-foot limestone Jesus, the Meat Packers Union's surviving members relive their union strike and beefy youth. Over the past twenty years, all but two members have become meat for the worms. My Grandfather, Braulio "Pepper" Luis Cantero, and his fellow meatpacker Sean Sermon Williams are the only two members alive. But unknown to me at that time, as we cruised down the highway listening to Ramon Ayala, soon there would be one less surviving member of the 61' Meat Packers strike.

Into Oblivion

I spent the morning fighting off this horrible maldita-cruda hangover. I got home at four, went straight to the restroom, and yacked all over the toilet. It was one of those rare moments where I had to take a shit at night. Still, as I sat there, the room slowly spun like a horrible rollercoaster that goes in circles to music from the eighties. The Scrambler. The kid at the controls slowly kicked the ride into overdrive. I threw up all over the place. The toilet bowl is full of my stinking shit and vomit. As I kneel there half-naked, with shit still crusting my butt cheeks like peanut butter between two slices of bread, I realize I must change my wicked ways. Then much to my horror, the toilet won't flush.

At nine in the morning, somewhere between my sweats, my buzz-saw headache, and the few moments of sleep I can muster, I receive a phone call from my uncle, Jesus. I don't answer it. I'm in too much pain to deal with his bullshit. Instead, I throw my phone against the wall, and it stops ringing.

At one in the afternoon, I make an effort to wake up, but the action is laced with laziness. At one point, I put on my shades to avoid the relentless desert sun. I get up to wash my face, feel defeated, and fall back into bed.

By the time I get to my cell phone, I've missed twenty-three calls, all from Jesus.

"Charlie, where the fuck you at?" His recorded

voice screams over the tiny speaker in my phone.

Two messages later, I discover that Pepper is in the hospital. They took him to Vista Del Sol.

I call Jesus. He doesn't answer.

The hangover over pounds on my head. My skull is a bone drum. My dry mouth keeps me from swallowing the knot forming in the dry thorny desert of my throat.

Pepper's going to be alright, I keep telling myself.

I call my ex, Julie. She'll understand the situation. She'll give me a ride. I get her voice mail. Fuck it. I hoof straight to the bus stop. I'm ablaze in the summer sun. The entire city is melting, cooking us all with it. My brain boils over in the oven of my shaved scalp. By the time I get to the bus stop, I'm two shades darker. Baked.

He's alright.

He's alright.

He's alright.

The bus doors open, and a burst of hot air smacks me in the face, and the queef joke I always make is replaced by thoughts of my grandfather dying at Vista Del Sol. I have to keep positive. The doctors are making a case for cutting back on bacon, coffee, sweet bread, or any number of vices. He has diabetes, but he's fit. He even exercises while in bed by kicking his bony legs up into the air. He stretches his lower back until his spine pops.

I sit in the plastic mold seating. My jeans are sticky with the late-night stink of booze and cigarettes. But they were the cleanest jeans I had. As the bus pushes onto the freeway, I can't help but think of the red spit I splattered all over the sink when I brushed my teeth. I spit blood like a boxer, and last night had been bloody. But before I can dig too deep into my bullshit, the image of Pepper dying keeps bouncing me back to my grandfather. My buddy.

He's alive.

He's alive.

He's alive.

I've never been more sure of anything in my life. I'm not a pessimist.

The bus routes, highlighted in reds and greens on the bus map, remind me of veins pumping through the endocrine system of El Paso, the Sun City. The forty-six goes direct to Vista del Sol. Three people were waiting at the stop when the bus pulls up at the bus stop in front of the hospital. Six of us get off.

I know Pepper's laughing right now. Making fun of Jesus, calling him fat. Or maybe he's drinking apple juice with a tray of gray hospital food in front of him.

Pepper is in good shape.

He wakes up at five every morning for walks in the park. My grandfather lives a healthy life. He doesn't drink anymore. He can push mowers over green lawns.

He swings axes at ugly mesquite trees. He drops concrete to level the earth. No way he's dying. He's probably watching a fight on the twelve-inch television in the corner of the hospital room. Hospitals have cable, right?

Of course, I pray. *Please, God, keep Pepper alive, and I promise I'll change. My life for his.* I'm not sure what I promise to change. I will be a better person. I'll spend more time with my family. I'll stop drinking, stop fornicating, stop smoking weed, stop snorting coke, stop dropping ecstasy, and stop shrooming. But all that doesn't matter. Not today.

Two male nurses push a pruned woman attached to an IV into the cold hospital elevator. I flatten against the wall to give them room. I try not to look at her, but the mirrors on the ceiling and walls reflect the woman's tiny, shriveled frame. Even her bones have pruned. She breathes and wheezes dust. Pepper can't be in this bad shape. I get off first, squeezing past the nurses and the old woman. My hand grazes her shoulder. I thought she'd be cold, a frozen stiff, but her skin felt soft, rice paper-thin but soft. The warmth pushing off of her gave me hope. Pepper's okay.

When I enter the room, Zeus and Monse stand over Pepper like vultures. They are ready to tear his carcass apart. They both turn and give me the Cantero stare, bunched-up eyebrows and slits for eyes. I smell like hungover raw ass, but neither Hey-Zeus nor Monse say anything. I hug Monse first, then Zeus. Pepper's eyes open, and for a moment, my hope turns into trust. I trust he's still alive. I trust he can recover. But his brown irises roll up into the back of his head. My Grandma pushes his eyelids shut, but they spring open when she lets go of them.

"I've been trying to shut them all morning," she says.

Zeus puts his heavy hand on my shoulder and squeezes hard. "He's had a stroke. Charlie, no oxygen to the brain." Zeus's voice stresses over his tears as he hugs me hard and heavy, like he wants to squeeze the life out of me.

Monse won't stop sobbing. I help her to a chair. I go to the nurses' station to get help. Monse sags into the chair, and the white of her eyes go hazy and bloodshot with tears.

A nurse brings her two white pills, a plastic cup of orange juice, and a blood pressure cuff. He velcros the cuff around Monse's arm, then pumps the black rubber ball until the cuff swells. The nurse checks the gauge and releases the valve. It hisses like a tiny viper.

"Miss Cantero, would you like to lie down?" the nurse asks.

The nurse runs his slender fingers through his curly red hair. Monse shrugs snorts, and laughs.

"Maricón," she snarls.

He apologizes for not speaking Spanish, removes the blood pressure cuff, and tucks it under his armpit. "She's fine," he says.

Monse laughs at him again. I squeeze her shoulder, a hint to be quiet, but she doesn't shut up. She embarrasses the nurse, but he stands there, red and sweaty, explaining Pepper's condition. Monse looks up at him and digs her nails into the chair.

"No, me siento bien," Monse growls between her clenched dentures. "Maybe I should be in a hospital bed next to Pepper."

For as long as I can remember, Monse has claimed to be dying. When I was a child, she told me she had cancer. Once, while in high school, I asked if I could join the wrestling team, and she told me that she had a heart condition and could die from worrying about me. She needed me home. I joined anyways and lost every single match that year. She had cursed me. When I told her I wanted to leave El Paso after graduating high school, she asked if I could stand being so far away from her. She said she would die because my leaving El Paso would kill her.

For a moment, I wished she was in the hospital bed instead of Pepper. I had to drive that thought out of my head. The nurse explains that Pepper has lost ninety-eight percent of his brain functions.

Monse, Zeus, and I all grab hands. We pray. Monse's whispers and mantras fall in rhythm with the clicks and beeps of the machines keeping Pepper alive.

We pray hard, offering ourselves as a sacrifice. We promise God our lives and devotion. Just bring Pepper back. But Pepper's brain has died, and I know only a dried corn husk remains. We move our prayer circle over to Pepper. He's lying there, mouth wide open and stuffed with plastic tubes. His lips have crusted from the cold air unit cooling the room.

Monse cups his jaw in her palm and keeps his mouth shut around the breathing tube. She holds an onyx rosary over his face. The rosary nestles between his mustache and his nose. She prays in low tones that gather in her chest and boil over in her throat. Deep thunderous rumbles that sound heavy like a train passing by.

I half expect a miracle. But nothing comes.

A squat and hairy doctor enters the room. He looks down at his clipboard and flips through the pages. The doctor explains that we can keep Pepper as a brain-dead vegetable or pull the plug. Jesus makes the call. Put Pepper down. I will forever hate him for that.

We all stay in the room as a team of nurses remove Pepper's breathing tube from his throat. Pepper trembles, his last movement on Earth. The machine tracking his heartbeat goes flat. They drain the fluid in the IV. The liquid goes into a baby blue plastic bag with a bright red biohazard sticker.

"Would you like to say your goodbyes?" one of the nurses asks.

Monse's cries are hysterical. I pull her into the hallway. I hug her, then Jesus joins us soon after. The three of us hug tight, forming a cocoon into which we weep.

Dracula vs El Burro

Even the cicadas would quiet their insipid rattling long enough to hear Monse spin one of her tales. Her stories stick to your bones and could haunt you years after she told them.

Monse told stories about farm animals, cattle rustlers, the moon and the stars, Aztec stories, and ancient world stories of Christ and Muhammad. Still, of all her stories, none did I love more than Dracula, and when she told it, a shadow would fall over her face. She reminded me of the old gypsy telling Lon Chaney that he had the curse of the Werewolf. Between her sentences and pauses, I fall in love with language and metaphor.

She always started Dracula by gnashing into the baby fat of my arm.

"Do you want to hear the story of Vlad the Impaler?" Her voice would grumble low and throaty. "He wants to suck your blood, Sharlie." Gnash, gnash, "and kill you."

I'd tuck into bed, my hair still wet from the bath she had given me. She would follow behind me, tucking herself in next to me nice and tight. Her body felt like a heater. On a cold desert night, I welcomed her. I slept close to the wall in the summer to feel the cold surface against my legs and forehead. Either way, hot or cold, I listened to every word until one of us fell asleep.

One night, when she seemed more tired than usual, her shoulders heavy and her eyes half-open, she fell asleep in the middle of Dracula's story. She drifted away on a particularly gruesome scene where Dracula had murdered the entire crew on the ship. Blood was dripping from his mouth. Dracula's fangs and nails were covered in flesh and connective tissue. The deck was covered in gore, and sharks circled the boat, enticed by the chum made from the crew. Only the Captain remained. Dracula stalked the Captain to the stern of the boat. Where the captain had fallen to his knees and prayed the sailor's prayer. "Now I lay me down to sleep. I pray the Lord my soul to keep. Grant that before I wake, no other sailor my shoes and socks will take. Lord, watch over me."

Dracula opened his jaws wide until they became unhinged like a python's jaw. His fangs gleamed under the moonlight. The waves of the Black Sea slapped against the schooner. Sharks swam in a frenzy around the boat, lured by what remained of the crew. Dracula's cold, pale hand gripped the Captain by the neck and lifted him to his feet. The Captain prayed louder, begging God for forgiveness.

"God has abandoned you," snarled Dracula in a heavy Eastern European accent.

But before Dracula could sink his teeth into the Captain, Monse let out a booming snore.

I held onto my little brown balls in anticipation. At first, I thought Monse had snorted as part of the story like maybe Dracula had made that noise before tearing into the handsome Captain's neck. Then she let out another snore, followed by a lighter, higher-pitched snort. I turned around to look at Monse. Her eyes had rolled back, her lids closed three-quarters of the way, and her mouth gaping open. I could see the black of her cavities and the gap of her missing teeth. I tried to fall asleep too, but the pounding of my heart rang in my ears, and the wind whistled and shook the window. I thought it was Dracula scratching at the window. I nudged Monse on the side of her boob. She rustled for a second, then went back to snoring. All the while, the deep desert winds clashed against the window. Dracula was here, baring his fangs, ready to twist my neck and bite into my boy's flesh. I yelled Monse's name and elbowed her in her enormous left breast. It jiggled like the mattress of a water bed.

Monse woke up startled. She put her hands up to protect her face and started yelling. Maybe she had been dreaming of being attacked by Vlad and his long bloody nails scraping at the window. But she was dreaming of my grandfather.

"What was I saying?" She asked.

"I don't know, Abuela, something about Dracula biting the last man on the ship. The brave Captain."

She rolled over so that we were back to back, rubbed the sole of her cold, thick feet against my feet, and continued her story.

"As the Captain cried out for his Mom, Dracula bit deep into his neck, past the tendons and muscle until he got to the Captain's neck bone." She let out another snore. I tapped her feet with mine, and she started back up like an old projector.

"The next night, Dracula arose to find the schooner swaying back and forth on the calming waves of the Black Sea. He had killed every man on that boat, and now the unquenchable thirst for blood pulled at his dead black heart. He sniffed the air, thinking he could smell people on land, but all he got was a whiff of salty sea and rotting seaweed. For a moment, Dracula thought about flying to the shore, but he feared he would not make land by dawn. *Oh, to see the sunrise once more, to see it crest over the water, bright yellow and furious, a vision almost worth the end of his existence,* he thought. But the hunger would not let him go, and he would never sacrifice himself, even for one last glimpse of God's glorious creation.

Dracula stared into the Black Sea, looking for his reflection in the black waters. But only the moon reflected back. He had not seen his reflection or the sun in centuries. He had long forgotten his sharp nose, broad chin, and almost feline eyes. As Dracula looked for his reflection in the water, he thought about the monster he had become, a beast set loose on this unforgiving world. He vowed to drain all life from this world until God herself came down from the heavens to beg Dracula to stop. He cursed God and God's fastidious rules of devotion and love. For Dracula had known only one love. Her name rolled off the tip of his forked tongue, "Elizabeth Bathory."

He cursed God for taking Elizabeth from him and swore to kill every creature created in God's image.

Suddenly, in the dead quiet of the night, among the soft calm of the ocean, and the unbearable thirst raging in his dead heart, he heard what he mistook to be a person breathing in the bowels of the ship. The noise was faint. A whisper. Perhaps a stowaway that he had missed. He followed the noise until he found a hatch on the ship's deck and opened it slowly. He wanted to savor his victim's fear, for he needed to keep this victim alive until the boat reached land.

Dracula could hear the strong and fast-beating pulse of a young heart. A smile stretched across his blood-stained lips, exposing his fangs. *A child*, he whispered into the night air. What else could have such a strong heartbeat? He climbed down the latter, salivating more and more. Children were the best blood meal because their hearts were still pure, uncorrupted by the world's greed. Children were his favorite to tear apart because God favored them.

Dracula crawled on the ship's floor as to not startle the child. He saw it moving in the corner of the stall, rustling about in the hay. He thought about scaring the child because the adrenaline would make the heart pump faster, and the blood would flow out in intense spurts, a perfect fountain of life. Dracula howled and barked until the entire bowel of the ship filled with what sounded like a pack of wolves. The hay moved about. Dracula unhinged his jaws and lept for the child. Only the creature he mistook for a child was a brown donkey in the hay.

The donkey flapped its lips and shook its massive head as if to say to Dracula, why are you disturbing my sleep. Dracula gnashed his fangs in anger. The donkey arose, lifting its massive head, which Dracula had mistaken to be a child huddled in the hay. The donkey extended its raspy tongue and scooped up some hay. He took a long chew.

Had Dracula not been so greedy and left one or two crew members alive, he would have had no need for the Donkey. Animal blood meal tasted foul to the undead. Still, Dracula needed blood. And the donkey's thick throbbing artery called to Dracula's deepest impulses.

Unable to control his urge, Dracula lunged at the donkey's neck. The donkey spun to the right and struck Dracula in the chest with its glorious brown rump. Dracula fell back, landing six feet from the donkey. The donkey chewed on more hay.

Dracula's eyes bulged, and his fangs glistened with drool. Again, he lunged at the donkey. Again, the Donkey spun around and knocked Dracula back to the floor.

Dracula sat on the floor amazed, but the donkey went on chewing its hay.

It was unclear to Dracula what upset him more, the donkey that had knocked him down or that, despite all the howls and barking, the donkey remained unafraid.

Dracula sat on the floor, watching the donkey's jaw muscles contract and ripple. The animal's hoof tapped on the wood floor. The beast had rhythm.

A fly flew near the donkey's rump, and the donkey swatted it away. The fly landed a few feet from the Donkey and kicked and sputtered until it died.

Dracula grew furious. He stood, stretched his arms out, and howled. The skin of his arms fell to his legs making giant wings. His eyes turned black, and fur grew all over his body. His mouth and nose stretched into a snout that resembled a wolf. Dracula screamed out a roar and stomped the floor, hoping to scare the donkey. But the donkey continued chewing his hay, undisturbed.

Rabid with fury, Dracula flew at the beast. The donkey spun around, lifted its hind leg, and smashed its hoof into Dracula's snout. Dracula flew back into the corner of the stall. He held his wings up to his bleeding mouth, and his howls became the whimpers of a hurt animal. Then he noticed something hard, smooth, and wet in the folds of his wings, but the tears in his eyes kept him from seeing the object. He transformed from a winged creature back to a man. His vision was blurry, and his hand trembled as he opened his fist. At first, he couldn't make out the white object in his palm, but his vision cleared. With absolute horror, he saw his fang in his palm. The donkey turned back around, flapped its lips in a loud bray, and chewed on some more hay. The one-fanged Dracula squeezed the fang in his palm, and with fury burning in his eyes, he lunged at the donkey again. He would have it, this donkey's blood. He would drain it of every last drop. Dracula flew at the donkey, and just as Dracula was about to sink his one good tooth into the donkey's neck. The donkey sprung its head to the sky, launching Dracula through the boat's deck. Dracula crashed through the deck. The wood shards splintered into his arms and legs. He landed on the deck, stabbed, cut, and pierced. Off in the distance, he saw the mighty burning hot sun rise over the Black Sea for the first time in centuries.

My eyes were wide open. I had never heard of the donkey that killed Dracula. I always thought Van Helsing had driven the stake through Dracula's black heart.

"Do you know the lesson of that story?"

My mind raced for the answer, "Don't be greedy?"

"No, *pendejo*," she said. "Even a burro can fight back."

How We Bury Our Dead

We can have my Grandfather memorialized on a plush felt blanket for ninety-two dollars and ninety-nine cents. I'm talking about the type of heavy felt blankets adorned with Aztec calendars or white tigers you see hanging at swap meets in south El Paso. We can also have his image etched in silver, glass, and gold or get a wood plaque with his image burnt onto oak or walnut. These are all options, add-ons, or souvenirs as part of platinum funeral packages available at Perches Funeral Home.

After the balding salesman makes his pitch, he tells Monse, Zeus, and I that the coffin used in the cremation is not included in the price of the funeral package. He hands my uncle another catalog. On the high end of burning coffin options is a cedar coffin that lends a sweet aroma to the cremated remains. The caskets range from cedar to double-thick corrugated cardboard. The cardboard coffin costs four hundred dollars. Four hundred dollars for a cardboard box!

"I'll give you all a minute," he says in Spanish. "Don't forget to look at the Tokens of Remembrance." He winks at me and rushes out the door to answer his cell phone.

This is how we bury our dead. In a cluster-fuck of overpriced mementos. But my grandma isn't buying it. She's from the rancho and isn't swayed by glossy catalogs, shiny souvenirs, or greasy salesmen. She skips on the felt blanket, the engraved glass, and the cedar coffin. She points to the cardboard box for the cremation and a modest brown leather-covered box for Pepper's remains.

The salesman returns, apologizes for stepping out, and then reviews our request form. He places the document in front of Monse.

"You sure you don't want any of the mementos?" He shoots Jesus a smile. "I'm sure your Mom would love to have a blanket with..." The salesman looks down at his phone, "Braulio's face on it."

"Clearly, you don't know our mom."

Monse slams her hand on the table so hard that the mementos around the room shake.

The sweaty salesman puts his hand together as if he's about to pray. I ask him to give us another minute.

When the salesman leaves Monse, Jesus and I start laughing. That poor bastard must've seen my Grandma and thought, *here's some easy prey, a shriveled little old lady and her two sons.*

I'm meeting cousins and aunts at Pepper's funeral, whom I've never met. Beautiful Mexican women dressed in black and pressing against me, sobbing into the nape of my neck. I have to admit, I got a little aroused. But I don't like to remember it that way, me perving on my dead grandpa's Mexican relatives. I'm sure if Pepper was alive, he would've laughed at seeing me flustered by these women.

You can tell who the Canteros are. Pepper's blood relatives share the same crispy deep brown amber skin, tight squinting eyes, and small round heads. Most are from Zacatecas, but some came from Aldama, where Pepper and Monse had lived before coming to El Paso.

The surviving Amalgamated Meat Packers' Union members sit in the back. Pepper had become the head of the El Paso chapter after the strike and held that position until he retired in the eighties. Most of them are big burly Mexican men married to big beefy women. And Pepper liked the beef. When a thick busty woman walked past us, he'd give me a sharp elbow to my ribs so I'd notice him noticing the woman's chi-chis. For example, suppose a heavy-set woman bent over to get her newspaper or tended her garden. In that case, he'd honk his truck's horn and yell "nalgame Dios!" or "Chi-chi's Christ," which always cracked me up.

When Pepper was alive, he attended mass for salvation and forgiveness. But seeing women dressed to the nines in polyester skirts and matte-black high heel shoes helped him become a Church regular. He loved women in the cardinal sense.

Both the priest and the coffin are loaners from the funeral home. Neither Monse, Jesus, nor I knew what church Pepper went to on Sundays, so we couldn't find his Priest.

This Priest's heavy European accent makes his Spanish hard to understand. His words are rolled in heavy R's, and all the S's are flattened with TH's. While sitting in the pews, listening to this guy fumble through the bible, my mind wanders first to the lender coffin, then to the cross hanging over it. I wish I had gone with Pepper to at least one mass. Unlike most Catholics, Pepper never pushed God on us, never got judgmental, and kept from preaching to us. He did like his crosses, though. Pepper had so many crosses on the wall that you'd think he was protecting himself from vampires or even the Devil himself. Every morning he prayed to those crosses, and the little suffering Jesus Christs, stretched out on the crosses, witnessed Pepper's devotion.

My favorite Catholic holiday was Ash Wednesday because I'd spend hours ragging on Pepper when he came home from Mass with ashes smeared across his head. "Hey, quien te quemo? Guey." I'd laugh, pointing to the cross of ashes smeared across his forehead. Or I'd grab one of the crosses from his room, put it on his forehead, and declare that he was evil. The ashes were proof the cross had burnt him. He'd laugh too and corner me, pretending to box me, tapping my lonjas and laughing as I kept my guard up. That's how I like to remember him, laughing. His bright silver tooth gleaming in the sunlight.

Though Monse hated crosses, religion, and Catholicism, she never gave Pepper a hard time for his religious devotion. We all hated those little crosses in Pepper's room, but like Monse, we never gave him a hard time about his faith. The crosses were wicked little reminders of the foul nature of humanity. Little suffering Christs with their arms outstretched and pinned back so that he would forever have to embrace us with open arms.

It surprised me when Monse requested a priest for Pepper's funeral. Truth be told, my uncle and grandmother had no faith in Pepper's faith. But Catholicism kept him from the booze, and for that, they were grateful. Monse and Jesus knew him before he had turned to Christ when he was a ruthless drunk. They knew the heavy-handed blurry-faced monster that would bruise their backs, thighs, and arms on particularly heinous nights.

By the time Pepper and Monse had adopted me, Pepper had quit drinking. He sealed that bitter demon into a leak-proof casket. He had found the lord, and the lord had saved him. His sobriety had left him a kind man, patient, and steady. The Dr. Jekyll to his Mr. Hyde, that had punched out Monse's front teeth and whipped his chubby cherub son with a bright orange extension cord. No, that was not the Pepper I knew. He never laid a hand on me. But that didn't stop Monse from keeping that blurry-faced booze monster alive in the bedtime stories she whispered into my ear. And in my tiny little ear canal, he'd stomp around with his fists clenched, wild-eyed, and frothing at the mouth.

Once, while in the middle of a story about her cousin, Markito, she got so pissed that she sprang out of bed, went to the kitchen, grabbed a carton of eggs, and smashed it on Pepper's head. I had gotten out of bed and stood in the hallway watching her charge back from the kitchen with the carton of a dozen extra large eggs. Pepper was asleep, his mouth open, his snore quiet and calm. Monse stood over him, her brow tensed, and her face became a storm of anger. She lifted the egg carton over her head and swung down all executioner-like. She wanted to take his head off. The carton smashed, crashing against the crown of Pepper's bald head. He squirmed and jumped to his feet, nearly clipping his head on the ceiling fan. His face was covered in yoke.

"Por que?"

She extended her crooked middle finger, flipping him off. "For Markito," she growled.

Pepper looked at me standing in the doorway and shook his head no before wiping away the yoke. She cocked the busted carton back, ready to swing at Pepper again. He flinched and brought his arms up to defend himself.

"Puto," she said in a low tone as if it were a secret.

The thought of my grandfather standing on his bed, covered in yoke, makes me laugh pretty fucking hard, and for a moment, I forget that I'm at his funeral. The priest gives me the evil eye, then continues his blah-blah-blah sermon. Monse digs her fingers into my thigh and claws into my flesh. A pain jolts up the right side of my body, and I stop laughing.

My mind keeps pushing against the sad sight of Pepper lying in the casket. The make-up artist made him two shades too white, and the fluorescent lights aren't helping. I need to run out of the funeral home. I need to scream and curse. I need to rage. So I stand up to walk out, but Monse grabs my sweaty hand. Her hand's warmth draws me closer to her. I hug her, then pull away. She lets me go, and I hurry outside.

The cold air fills my lungs and calms me. The sunsets over the purple and brown desert mountains to the west. If I squint hard enough, I can almost make out the forty-two-foot statue of Christ on top of mountain Christo Rey. His arms opened wide, embracing the United States and Mexico.

Once a year, Pepper and the other Amalgamated Meat Packers involved in the 61' strike would pilgrimage up Mount Christo Rey and pray at the feet of the limestone Jesus.

Sometimes I made that hike up the mountain with him, more so when I was a kid, but he'd invite me every year, even when I moved out of the house. I'd usually turn him down on account that I was too hungover. As a kid, Pepper would wake me before dawn while the rest of the world slept, and the sun would crack open the valley in those hours. I felt loved in those moments. I felt safe. The two of us readying ourselves to climb a mountain, to stand before God like some grand adventure. In those moments, as I watched Pepper prepare our lunches, pack our bags and fill the thermos with coffee, I learned that Men could be careful and gentle. That our motions could be sweeping and graceful too. I realized that the hard-working, callused exterior was all for show. Men could be kind.

We'd listen to Ramón Ayala's cassettes on the way

to Mt. Christo Rey. 'Tragos Amargos' was Pepper's favorite. The fresh desert morning would fog up the window, and I'd hold the thermos between my thighs to keep warm. The defroster would clear up the windows by the end of the first song. There is magic in the early morning, the sun rising, the window defrosting, and the world looking bright and new. Pepper would push in the clutch, and we'd coast down the freeway. The stars still cascaded behind the Franklin Mountains, slowly fading away from the sun rising over the east. We were cruising through space while listening to Ramon rip on his accordion. I'd close my eyes and drift across the galaxy until I found that delicate veil between sleep and being awake.

Pepper would startle me by nudging me in the ribs as we approached the mountain. I'd jump, and Pepper would flash me a big ole grin. The silver lining of his false teeth shined and glimmered from the early morning sun.

After that climb up Mt. Christo Rey, I felt different. I had become a man for braving the desert mountains, feeling the cactus' thorns pierce my ankles, tasting the desert dust, and sweating under the Spring sun. This was our right of passage.

Pepper and I were parched and bloody when we reached the top of Christo Rey. We'd sit at the top of the mountain and stare at the beautiful desert expanding into the muscular mountains that shape the valley. I could see El Paso and Juarez, and Sunland Park. The muddy banks of the once-mighty Rio Grande River sealed together three states and two countries. We'd eat the warm fluffy eggs and beans wrapped in Monse's homemade flour tortillas. Then, in timed increments, the remaining Amalgamated Meat Packers would show up, some with their sons, others with a wife or girlfriend, though most came alone.

The church bells ring, and they snap me out of the memory. When I return to the front pew in the funeral parlor, I find Monse crying up a hysterical storm. I feel the guilt creep up my spine. I want to run back outside, but the priest motions me to sit. Waiting for the priest to finish his sermon becomes a long torturous ordeal. The microphone keeps popping and clipping, forcing the priest to stop every couple of sentences to adjust the clip-on microphone attached to his chasuble. He fumbles with it for a few minutes, then eventually gets the microphone off from around his neck and holds it in his dainty hand. Why do priests always have dainty hands?

My grandma pulls her lace shawl across her shoulders and drapes it over her head. She cries into her hands, and I want to hug her, comfort her, and take her pain away, but instead, I sit there and sob too.

At the end of his sermon, the priest waves his hand over Pepper's coffin and presents Pepper to the crowd as if the whole thing were part of a magic act. Ashes to ashes, dust to ta-da!

The blue fibers in Pepper's gray suit shimmer under the fluorescent bulbs hanging over his coffin. His mustache and hair are dyed black. A bolo tie, with a silver arrowhead encrusted in turquoise stones, lays on his chest.

The priest invites Jesus, Monse, and I up to the coffin. We cry and hold on to each other as if we are afraid to lose each other in a large crowd. My grandma huddles over Pepper's coffin and cups his face as she did in the hospital the day he died. She cries into his chest. His cold gray suit muffled her cries.

My uncle scoops her up from the side of the coffin, but she screams and kicks and curses in broken English and broken Spanish. I try to help, but Zeus waves me back to the coffin.

"Stay with the family."

Those in attendance have lined up in the center aisle to give their last goodbyes and to get one last glimpse of Braulio "Pepper" Cantero. One by one, as if in a buffet line of grief, they look over the casket before hugging me and expressing their condolences. The whole procession takes fifteen minutes, and finally, I'm the last one in the parlor. Before I leave, I kiss Pepper on the corner of his cold lips. He smells like cedar and anise, and his skin feels like cold chicken meat.

"I love you, Cabron," I whisper into his ear.

This is how we bury our dead. This is how we say goodbye.

Everybody's Grandpa Gets Lit at Chacha's

"Pepper was seventeen when they murdered his brother," Monse said one hot summer night as she picked me up to carry me to the bed. I had just gotten out of the bathtub, and my pruned toes and fingers were plumping up again. I was eight years old. I used to let my bath water run cold because it felt like a swimming pool. All my toys were in the tub with me. He-Man and a handful of plastic luchadores that Monse had bought me last week on our wait to cross from Juarez, Mexico, into El Paso, Texas.

The luchadores looked so grand in their packaging. The street vendor had twenty wooden wrestling rings, each with four luchadores. The four wrestlers were twisted up in the rubber bands that were the rope around the wrestling ring. The luchadores had bright yellow and blue painted-on masks. One of them had felt hair glued to its plastic scalp. They all had capes, but only one looked like Santos.

Every night for the past three weeks, the four luchadores have been battling He-Man during my bath. After the long hour-and-a-half battles, I would prune up and call for Monse to take me out of the tub. Monse would come in with a towel to pull me out of the tub. I loved to watch the dirty water and defeated wrestles twirl in the whirlpool of the drain, punishment for losing to He-Man. "Para la otra," they yelled as they circled the drain.

"Though Pepper was a scrawny little guy, not much bigger than you are now, he had a mustache since he was eleven and was very proud of it. His mustache and an older brother that everybody respected gave Pepper a sense that he was muy Chingon," Monse said as she dried me off. "He had a mouth on him. And it got him into plenty of trouble." Then she paused and looked me in the eyes. "That's why it is better to listen than to be a big mouth."

I toweled off, put on my underwear, and jumped into the bed. I knew it was going to be a good story. Monse took her time getting into bed. Her movements were deliberately slow because she had my attention. She savored every moment until I begged her to tell me the story of the death of Palacio Hernan Wiso Cantero.

"Pepper was at Chacha's, a dirty little bar on the outskirts of Aldama. 'She's very cochóna,' Pepper said, running his mouth." Monse tried her best to imitate Pepper's voice, which was softer than Monse's because she had smoked for many years. She returned to her story. "Pepper ordered a beer and shot of Scotch as a group of old toothless barflies gathered around to hear him tell his story. The barflies fed off stories, trying their hardest to relive some part their youth long lost at the bottom of a bottle.

'Le gusta verga,' Pepper shouted as he raised a glass.

Then he pumped his palm and winked at the

other piss-poor drunkards crowding around him. Even if they hadn't cheered him on, it didn't matter to Pepper. He kept on bragging about what he did to this poor girl.

As the drunks clanked their piss-warm beer and laughed, there was this man with a sour look on his face. He had a thick neck and skin dark as mahogany. His eyes were bloodshot, and the sun had beaten his leathery face. His mad dog eyes were fixed on Pepper, who, for his life, couldn't stop bragging about this girl's culote and chichotas.

'I thumbed her little culo.' His voice was jovial and gleeful as he wagged his thumb.

The men laughed. 'What's her name?' they shouted.

'Esmeralda, guey,' Pepper said to the guy closest to him. 'Esmeralda Dos Lobos,' Pepper jeered. The jaws dropped on everybody in the bar, including the waitress. Pepper was too drunk to notice and kept on with his story. One by one, the barflies slowly moved away from Pepper.

'Then my brother gave me this beautiful little twenty-two to commemorate the evening,' Pepper bragged.

As Pepper reached into his boot and pulled out the Sentinel .22 his brother had given him, the fat-headed, sun-burnt, thick-necked Mexican sitting in the darkest corner of the bar slammed his shot glass on the table, bounced to his feet, and charged at Pepper. The drunkards split like the red sea, giving that fat bastard a clear path to Pepper. He snatched Pepper up by the throat, lifting him clean out of his boots.

"That's my little sister, you fucking puto." The man was rabid with hate.

None of the barflies wanted anything to do with Esmeralda's brother, Cuero Dos Lobos, so they scattered. But they all watched as Cuero tried to turn Pepper into a stain on the bar's dirt floor.

Cuero slapped Pepper so hard that Pepper passed out, pissed his pants, and then woke up again when he felt the warm pool gather beneath him. Cuero stomped down, and Pepper curled up like one of those tiny dried shrimps that come with a hot sauce packet. Sure, Pepper tried his best to avoid the beer bottles and chingasos raining down on him, but it felt like every blow landed on his skull, ribs, or kidneys. His heart pounded in his chest, and his breathing was labored through the blood in his mouth and nose. Pepper saw no way out of this situation. He would have to take his beating like a man. Hopefully, someone in the bar would stop Cuero before he killed Pepper. Pepper had just turned seventeen, and his luck as a young man had turned for the worst.

Between the punches and stomps, Pepper recalled his brother telling him not to be so braggadocio. But it was too late, and unless his brother were to walk in and give Cuero what-for, Pepper was a dead man. That's when Pepper remembered the Sentinel .22 revolver in his boot. He reached for it, but Cuero's boot heal crashed down on Pepper's ribs.

'Auxilio,' Pepper yelled.

Before everything went black again, Pepper swore he heard his brother's voice. Then Cuero swung his leg back and let a kick fly into Pepper's face. Goal! and everything went dark.

One of the barflies must've splashed his beer on Pepper's face because Pepper came to and saw his brother standing over him.

'Levantate, guey,' Pepper's brother, Palacio, said.

Pepper sat up slowly. His brain felt like pulp. Cuero lay on the floor next to Pepper. Cuero's face was a smear of blood. The Sentinel .22 was next to Pepper, but he did not notice it. Palacio removed his belt and used it to whip Cuero's limp body. The leather belt lacerated Cuero's face and left welts on his arms.

'Levantate guey.'

The belt thundered and cracked as the barflies yelled and hollered like a bunch of hyenas. They wanted blood. They wanted a sacrifice. Pepper worked his way up to his feet. He gulped down a glass of liquor and turned to his brother.

'Stop, Palacio. You're going to kill him.' But his brother wouldn't stop. He kept whipping and kicking Cuero.

Cuero squirmed on the floor, then stood up and lunged toward Pepper. All the while, Palacio was punching him in the face and whipping him with the belt.

Then a gunshot rang out. Everyone stopped, and the room went silent.

Pepper ran his hands along his body, feeling for a wound. He was sure Cuero had shot him. Cuero stumbled like a top, losing its momentum before toppling over. Cuero clenched his gut and squealed in pain before falling to the floor.

Pepper's face had swollen, and he couldn't see from his left eye. He reached for the gun in his boot but lost it in the scuffle. He tried to look for it on the floor, but his swollen eye limited his vision. Pepper's lungs were on fire, and his hair and mustache were wet and sticky with blood.

Cuero had curled up and was moaning with pain. Pepper hawked a bloody loogie at Cuero's face and then kicked him in the gut where blood had pooled. Cuero grunted in pain. Pepper unleashed a barrage of kicks, all aimed at Cuero's fat head and his fat face. Cuero held to his gut with one hand and tried to cover his head with the other.

An idea dawned in the fog of Pepper's cloudy mind. He wanted to humiliate Cuero and teach the rest of the town never to mess with Braulio "Pepper" Cantero again. He unzipped his pants, whipped his dick out, and pissed all over Cuero. His foamy piss smelled like liquor and beer.

'What the fuck are you doing!' yelled Pepper's

brother.

Pepper spun around and saw his brother standing at the doorway with a .38 in hand. Palacio was a large man with broad shoulders. He took up the entire entrance.

'Let's go, pendejo. Andale guey!'

Pepper tucked away his schlong and ran to the exit.

'Puto,' grunted Cuero from the floor.

Pepper turned to get one last look at Cuero. Cuero lifted Pepper's .22 and fired the gun twice, and Pepper heard the bullet whiz by, but Cuero had missed him. Palacio pushed Pepper out of the way and put two more rounds into Cuero's gut, the .38 ringing the ears of all the barflies who had taken cover behind the bar stools and tables. Cuero groaned with each shot.

The two brothers ran out the door and headed to Palacio's car. Palacio threw Pepper the keys. 'That culo shot me in the leg,' Palacio said. 'You have to drive.'

Pepper tried to lift his brother into the car, but Palacio's meaty shoulders made him too heavy.

"Stop, Pendejo," said Palacio. "I can get myself into the car."

The engine turned over on the first try. Pepper pulled the car onto the dirt road and sped away. As they drove home, Palacio cursed that fat pig Cuero. 'Why are you bragging about his sister? Don't be a pendejo, guey.'

Palacio had stopped talking by the time they pulled up to the rancho.

'You okay, brother?' Pepper looked back at Palacio. Palacio's eyes were half shut, his mouth wide open. His skin had turned from a rich copper tan to a grey hue. Pepper jumped out of the car and pulled Palacio out of the sticky back seat. Palacio was too heavy, and Pepper dropped him next to the car. Pepper rolled Palacio onto his back. His brother's eyes were wide open now, and his mouth hung as if his last expression was of disbelief. Palacio had bled out, drained in the backseat of his 36' Hudson. Later, a doctor would confirm that Cuero's bullet had clipped Palacio's femoral artery."

I could not believe what Monse had told me about my sweet old Grandfather. I never saw him take a sip of booze, not at any of the backyard quinces, weddings, or birthday parties. He never touched the stuff and often looked disappointed with family and friends when they drank. He hated alcohol and would sign the cross whenever people offered him a drink.

I always thought his devotion to Catholicism motivated him to live clean. How could he be responsible for his brother's death? There's no way he had been a drunkard bragging to barflies. He was a pious man, a man of routine.

He'd wake up at five and pray before a wooden Jesus hanging from a crucifix. On the dresser, beneath the crucifix, Pepper had built an altar. The altar consisted of an old black-and-white picture of Pepper's mother and a plastic Virgen de Guadalupe filled with holy water.

I'd try to listen in on his prayers. He'd cry at the beginning of his oration, his voice cracking and shaky. By the end of his prayer, his voice would stabilize as if he had come to terms with something. I could only hear the sound of his syllables but never the whole language. His words came out fast, and they bled into one long word from which he would only stop to breathe. Only God could hear his mantra.

After his prayers, he'd take a long mean-shit and get ready for work.

She'll Use Her Words Like a Knife

On the ride from the funeral home back to Monse's house, we go through a cycle of emotion. We sob, then wipe away our tears, followed by deep heavy breaths. We repeat our cycle of grief over and over. We have lost control. Our bodies won't listen. Our tears blur the world. The lights from the cities of El Paso and Juarez stretch across the desert. The valley is a sea of stars, a blanket of galaxies that streak in our tears. My grandfather will never again see the beauty of these hot El Paso nights.

When we get to my grandmother's house, the neighbors help Monse out of Jesus's truck. Monse flings an arm around each of her comadres, and they all shuffle into the house together. They help her into the home like she's a boxer on her last leg, trying to find the corner.

They sit her at the table in the kitchen and feed her pumpkin empanadas, ham sandwiches, and warm creamed coffee. Monse has good neighbors and family friends eager to console her. Somehow food helps. She eats her tears as they soak into the empanada.

I walk into the kitchen, where they make room for me to sit next to my grandma, but I don't want to sit with these old hags. I don't want to listen to them talk about my dead grandpa. They insist I sit, and they lay a plate out in front of me. I bite the sandwich but can't taste anything because my senses are overloaded with the smell of old lady perfume. I tell them I have to use the restroom.

After escaping the gaggle of señoras, I'm pulled into a river of grief when I enter Pepper's room. Pepper didn't like the señoras much, either. He'd call them *viejas putas*, or *pinche viejas*. He would have kicked them all out if he had been alive.

I lie on Pepper's bed and close my eyes. I can hear people shuffling in the hallway. There's a mahogany crucifix on the wall, just above Pepper's bed, and Jesus, the son of God, not my fat uncle, looks down at me. He, too, grieves. Every morning, Pepper prayed to that mahogany Jesus nailed to his wall. That crucifix has always scared me, except for today.

"It's okay to be scared," Pepper once told me. "Jesus was scared too."

But before I can sulk and marinate on Pepper's memories and life, I hear the toilet flush in Pepper's bathroom. I go cold because Pepper died on that bathroom floor, and for a moment, I think he might be trying to reach out to me to give me a sign. The door creaks and opens slowly. The light frames the silhouette of a man.

"Charlie?" the shadow says.

"Pepper?"

"Sorry, man," says the figure in the doorway. "Do you have any toilet paper? I think those sandwiches and coffee got me."

As the man steps into the doorway, I see that it's

Omar, the son of Lencha, one of the neighbors.

I walk out without answering him.

As I pass the kitchen, my grandmother stretches her hand out and nods for me to come to her. Tears have smeared her eye shadow and mascara. Her makeup runs down her face, outlining her wrinkles. Her lipstick has gathered on the thin mustache highlighting her upper lip. I hug her, and she slobbers into my shirt, pulls me tight, and slobbers on me again. I let go of the little ball of pain in my chest, and the tears flow. I am pure emotion. A raw nerve, an exposed tooth. At that moment, Monse and I are the only ones in the room. Everyone else has become muted and blurred, deep shadows in the background of our hurt. The whole universe has gone quiet except for our sighs and sobs.

Eventually, she lets go.

"Eat something," she says.

The entire room comes back to life with the noise of condolences. The señoras echo my grandmother by encouraging me to eat. They offer enormous plastic trays of carrots, celery, and halved croissant sandwiches. I know I have to grab something, a celery stalk, a ham sandwich, or a piece of pound cake because my eating comforts my grandmother. It always has. I put a few shabby sandwiches on a paper plate and head for the front door.

Outside, Jesus's wife, Margie, sits in the opened hatch of her Honda CR-V with an ice chest of beers at her tan feet. The straps of her black patent leather sandals pull tight over her skin. I can't help but stare. She's wearing a silver toe ring on her middle toe. I gaze from her muscular calf, up the curve of her knee, and onto her thighs.

"We missed you at the funeral," I say in a desperate attempt to start a conversation.

She smiles and lights a cigarette.

"Your uncle wanted me to help," she says in a deep raspy, smoker's voice.

I'm all chub and semi-erect.

"Jesus said your grandma would be too tired to host. And that I should help with that. But as soon as Monse got home, she gave me that look. That you don't fucking belong, look. Figured it'd be best to stay out of her way."

I put two fingers up to my mouth to motion for a hit of her cigarette.

"They're menthols," she says.

"Just want a drag," I say. "Don't think I can smoke a whole one."

She hands me her lipstick-stained cigarette, and I am in heaven. I imagine our lips pressing against each other, the smell of menthol smoke and beer on both our breaths. I'm trying to taste her on the cigarette. It's moist.

I haven't smoked a cigarette in almost six months, not since a periodontist pulled a rotten tooth from my mouth and told me I had to quit smoking or lose all my teeth.

The menthol smoke shoots down my throat. It's cold in my lungs, leaving me queasy and needing to take a shit.

"It's not weed," Margie laughs.

I grab a beer and chug it. Then I crush the can and reach for another. The cold beer helps the pain in my stomach.

"Hey, take it easy," says Margie. "I don't want your grandmother getting pissed because I got you drunk."

"I can take the heat," I say.

"It's not you I'm worried about," she says. "Your grandmother hates me. I don't know why."

We both know that's a lie.

Three years ago, while visiting my grandma, I found Jesus crying over Monse's meaty shoulder. They were sitting in her living room, talking about how he had found pictures Margie had emailed to a co-worker.

Monse was crying too.

Margie's nasty pictures had torn my uncle's heart asunder, and only his mother could heal him. I sat on the couch next to them. I didn't know what to say. Half of me thought about those pictures, and the other half felt no sympathy for Jesus. Because Jesus was a dick and had cheated on Margie time and time again.

Margie's naked pictures were all I could think about for like two months straight. I imagined her tan, forty-year-old tits pushed up in a black lace bra. I spent days wondering what her labia looked like.

As we sit outside and I think of naked Margie, an image of Pepper rushes into my head and destroys the whole fantasy. I imagine him watering the pecan tree he planted in the front yard. I don't want to think about my dead grandpa, so I slam my second beer almost as fast as I had the first. I feel the buzz from the alcohol creep up my spine and into the base of my skull.

I tell Margie about work. I tell her about my girlfriend dumping my ass.

"She said she needed more," I say, hoping to get a sympathy hug. She doesn't fall for it, so I open beer number three and get at it.

"Let me give you some advice, Charlie," Margie says. "Your problem is that you," but before she can give me the advice, my uncle, Jesus, comes busting out of the house.

"It's getting heavy in there," Jesus says. "Mom won't stop crying. She says she wants to die too."

"You're getting heavy in there," I laugh.

"Watch it, chora face," Jesus says. "I'll fuck you up while Margie watches. Huh-Babe?"

He fakes two jabs into my gut, and I spill some of my beer.

Jesus drinks his beers almost as fast as I am chugging mine. I don't want to be here in this whirlwind of hot grief, and I'm sure Jesus doesn't want to be here either. We polish that twelve like it's happy hour.

"We need more beer," says Margie. Her hand is elbow-deep in the ice chest, looking for that hidden can. "I'll fly, you buy," she laughs.

I give her a ten, the last of my weekly money. I might have to sell more plasma tomorrow, but I don't want to worry about that tonight. I just want to get drunk. I want to be oblivion.

They leave for the gas station, and I stay outside and cry, staring at the big pecan tree in the front yard, its branches reaching up to the sky, reaching for Pepper. The tears blur my vision, and the memories of my youth bleed into the desert night. I can hear Pepper's voice. *Mijo, hechale ganas.* We toss a baseball back and forth, but I keep flinching when he throws the ball to me.

I want to stay with this memory, but a couple of neighbors walk outside and talk loud so I can hear them. I am yanked back to reality. I fucking hate neighbors. I return to the house before the neighbors tell me how sorry they are that Pepper has passed away. I don't want to hear it. What do they know of Braulio "Pepper" Luis Cantero?

Williams, Pepper's buddy from the Meat Packers Union, stands alone in the living room. He sticks out because he's about a foot and a half taller than the old Mexican ladies tending to my grandma. Also, he is the only black guy in the room. He has a thick mustache, not unlike my grandfather's mustache. Most of the older Meat Packer guys had the same mustache.

"Hey, Williams," I say as I approach him. "Thanks for coming."

"Charlie?" William's face lights up with a smile, and his mustache opens like angel wings. He shakes my hand. "Sorry about Pepper. He was a tough working son of a bitch." He looks me over. "Either way, it's good to see you, Charlie. How's work?"

That's the thing about these union guys; it's always about work with them.

"I do a little here and there. I guess. Mostly I cook at a restaurant downtown. Hours are good, but the pay, well, not so much." I shrug and look down at my empty beer can. "Jesus and his wife went to get some more beers. They'll be back soon."

I nod to the door, and he follows me outside to the front porch. He opens a box of Marlboro Reds.

"You smoke?"

I can smell the old nicotine on William's fingers as he hands me the cigarette.

He lights his cigarette and takes a deep drag. "I hope the money we gathered helps you and yours," Williams says. He exhales his smoke into the desert night.

"Money?" I take a drag but start coughing. "Whatcha talking about, Williams?"

"The money the Meat Packers gathered," he says. "You know the money we put together when one of us goes. We scraped just over six thousand for Pepper."

"It's the first I hear about it." I try not to act too eager. I'm not expecting anything from Pepper's will, but if they collected money for him and gave it to Monse, I won't feel so bad asking her to lend me money later in the week.

"We gave Jesus the money yesterday," Williams says. "I'm sure he used it for the funeral."

"Thanks. The family appreciates you guys."

Margie pulls onto Knight Street, and I hear her stereo playing Al Green's *Let's Stay Together* on full blast.

"God damn, I love this song!" Shouts Margie from the driver's seat as she pulls up the driveway. "I'm, I'm so in love with you, in any kind of weather, whether times are good or bad or happy or sad," she sings off-key and howls like a dog. Jesus reaches to lower her radio, but she slaps his hand. He looks her in the eyes then he motions to Monse's house.

"Oh, right," Margie says. She lowers the radio but not by much. Margie continues to sing as she exits the car and opens the hatch to her SUV. I open the box of beers, pour the cans into the cooler, and then hand out the beers.

"To my dad," says Jesus. "Damn, that son of a bitch liked to drink."

"I'm going to miss that old bastard," I say, then I chug half the beer. *Mister Blue Skies* comes on the radio next.

I bounce my head to the music, "Dang, Margie, this is good music."

"Thanks, it's a mix my co-worker made me." She pauses for a second, looks at Jesus, and then sings the song.

"Pepper would have hated this music being played at his wake," I laugh.

"You remember how you used to sneak into his room and play pranks on him?" says Jesus.

I'd love to take the batteries out of his remote, turn his TV on full blast, then turn the TV off. He'd come home from a long day at work, get undressed, and turn on the TV. The damn thing would blast so loud it would startle him. Then he'd try to use the remote to lower the TV's volume. Nothing. By the end of it all, he'd have the TV unplugged and would be cursing up a storm. "Pinche tele, vale verga esta cabrona."

Maybe because it's easier than crying, we all laugh.

"How about when he showed up to my baseball game drunk?" says Jesus. "He parked his yellow Maverick on the curb, behind the bleachers, honked, and hollered for seven innings. The coaches had to ask him to stop. 'Sir, this is a school event.' But Pepper gave zero fucks. Eventually, he passed out, and I had to drive us home after the game. I don't think I've been so embarrassed. I quit baseball after that shit."

Then Margie told her story about how Pepper came to her rescue when she blew a tire on the I-10 freeway. Jesus interrupted her by asking her where she was coming from that night. She didn't answer, so Jesus told us another story.

"You know I hate to say it," Jesus said. "But I think the old man is down below. I don't think you can be forgiven for killing family."

"Jesus! He was a good man." I say.

"Maybe by the time you came along, but you know how he treated Mom and me. Look, I love the bastard. I'm just saying our actions have consequences."

Margie looked a bit confused, or maybe she was just drunk. "When you put your dick on his forehead, that was plenty of pennance for his bullshit."

"Payback," says Jesus. "For all the times he busted Mom and me to shit."

"Yeah, I agree, but did you have to teabag your dad?"

"Of course," Jesus says.

We all knew the answer, Pepper was an asshole, and as a kid, I heard stories of Pepper's drunken days. I knew he had put a couple of beatings on Jesus and Monse.

"I could take the beatings, and so could Mom. What broke my heart was that every morning, no matter how bruised and swollen her face was, she always made him breakfast and packed his lunch." Jesus's eyes tear up.

We drink in unison, desperate to break the tension.

"He stopped after Markito died," Jesus says.

The night air cools, and we change the music to Chente Fernandez. Margie asks if I can get her jacket from inside the house.

"I don't think Monse wants to see me at all," she says.

When I walk into the house, Monse calls me over. She hugs me and soaks my cheek with tears and mucus. I turn away. A plaster bust of the upper half of Jesus Christ sits on the kitchen table. Jesus Christ is white, but his robe is trimmed in gold. His hands are stretched out as if receiving communion. The statue is staring up at me. I wonder who would gift such a retched and gaudy thing to Monse.

"Is that drunken perra, Margie, still outside?" Monse asks. "Why did she even come? She doesn't give a damn about Pepper." Monse wipes away the saliva from my cheek. "She goes where there's pisto and verga."

"At least she helped set up the house."

"Mijo, grow some huevos," Monse says. "Remind her that this isn't a bar."

"I will."

Monse sniffs the air, coyote style. "Are you drinking, too?"

"No, not one beer," I say.

"Cabrón," she slaps my arm. "You and that puta, me la van a pagar."

I grab Margie's jacket from the couch, smell it and rush outside. Williams is sitting on the red and white cooler, his fingers wrapped around a Bud.

"I hate to ask you this, Williams, but do you mind if I get a couple of brews?" I say. "Better yet, let me go get you a chair."

"Sure thing," Williams says.

I return with the chair. It takes ages for Williams to stand. His bones are wrecked from years of heavy factory work.

"This is what thirty years of carrying big meat will do to a guy," he laughs.

"Williams was telling me that he gathered money for Pepper's funeral," I say to Jesus.

"Yeah," Jesus says, "It helped out."

"I guess Monse must've forgotten or something," I say. "She asked if I could pitch in for the funeral costs."

"Wouldn't worry too much about it," Jesus says. "She's stressed, and I'm sure she ain't thinking straight."

We drink and cry until the sun rises over the mountains and light spreads across the valley. The silver ring wrapped around Margie's creamy coffee toe catches the light. At dawn, Jesus and I head inside. Margie passes out in the passenger seat. I motion to Jesus to pick her up and take her inside. But he tells me that she will be fine sleeping in the car.

I finally get to bed and hope to dream about Pepper. But I don't dream; there is only darkness, total and complete oblivion.

La Avispa

Monse pulled the blankets up to my chest, and I tucked myself into the folds of her enormous breasts. I must've been eight or nine at the time if I'm remembering. She pulled me in tight, but the smell of her perfumed baby powder made me push away.

"Ah si, Cabron," she said, then pulled me in tighter. I had to bury my face into the pillow to keep from smelling that baby powder. The smell made me nauseous, and years later, the scent of that perfumed powder would make my stomach knot.

"When I was a girl, living in Aldama," she said. "The chavos called me La Avispa." Her Northern Mexican accent was as heavy as cajeta, making it easy to fall asleep and dream the worlds she spun in her bedtime stories.

La Avispa's father, Lalo Jose de la Luna, ran booze through the Texas-Mexico border during prohibition. He made a small fortune delivering tequila, sotol, and mescal to the north. Lalo used the money to buy land in the town of Aldama. After the prohibition, Monse's family sold cattle, beans, rice, fresh farm eggs, milk, and Mennonite cheese. The children also got in on the family business of selling provisions. They made jamoncillo candies and paper mache puppets. My grandmother, La Avispa, worked at the smallest of the five family-owned puestos. Her store sold eggs and cheese. Her little store brought in the least money, but that changed after she turned twelve. Her puesto became the busiest of the family's puestos.

Lalo was no fool. He saw his daughter's transformation that winter, noting her glow, change in height, and the filling out of her blouse. It wasn't until one of his ranch hands asked Lalo for permission to court his daughter that it dawned on Lalo why the pueste was making money. He asked his oldest sons, El Gitano and Yucando, to watch Monse. "Stay close to her," he warned.

Monse, unlike her sisters, had inherited the same charm as her mother, Teresa. She turned down the fulanos who came calling but always did it with grace and a smile. Most of the boys backed down after the first no. No man wanted to dance with Monse's father. He was a hot-headed ferocious brawler, and his sons were known to be just as vicious. Besides, the boys in Aldama all looked like wet marsupials.

Then one day, Monse followed Julio Sebastian Garcia behind the schoolhouse. Julio had kissed her and rubbed up on her. This continued for a few days, and she liked the attention. Monse developed a sweet adolescent idea of marriage and children with Julio. Of course, she bragged to her sisters about her future husband. Then one day, Monse's father caught her kissing Julio behind the School House.

Lalo grabbed Julio by the back of the collar and slammed him to the ground. Then he slapped Monse across the face. His calloused hand left her dizzy, and she swore off boys for good. But eventually, the hand mark on her face, and fear of her Father faded away. She found herself sneaking away with her love and once again felt a deep to her core yearning for marriage and children. Her sisters told on her immediately.

Her father was waiting for her in the courtyard at the house entrance.

"Avispa, get in here." His voice throaty and firm.

She skipped over to him.

"Si, Papa?"

Her mind and soul were still at the schoolhouse, remembering the taste of Julio's squishy tongue and salty tamarindo lips. She was off daydreaming and missed the anger roaring in her father's face. She would've noticed his dark eyes, stressed brow, and ten-foot shadow cast on the wall behind him.

He didn't say anything.

He just watched her as she counted the petels on a sunflower, a gift from Julio.

"Mande, Papa?" She asked with a sigh.

Her father's callused hand slapped her across the face, and the thunderous clap echoed in the courtyard. She saw stars. The slap knocked the wind out of her, leaving her gasping for air. The slap landed so on point that it knocked the taste of Julio's tamarindo lips clean off her lips.

Her tears rolled down her red cheek, and her swollen face throbbed.

"Don't be a puta, Mija." His voice was firm but not angry. It was as if he were telling La Avispa to put away a toy or close the gate before the goats got out. She wondered if he had put all his anger and rage into that slap.

Later that night, over a bushel of burning sage, a candle of the Virgen de Guadalupe, and the crushed Sun-Flower Julio Sebastian Garcia had given her, La Avispa made a pact with her two older sisters to swear off boys for the rest of their lives. For Pina and Natty, the promise wasn't hard to keep. Neither of them had ever been courted. But for Monse, she couldn't walk down the street without being cat-called and whistled at. That night La Avispa looked out her bedroom window and asked God to let her relive the kiss with Julio, and she dreamed about the kiss. In the morning, she swore to her father that she would never kiss a boy again, but she crossed her fingers behind her back to nullify the promise.

Though she never kissed Julio again, she did find herself kissing a much older man. Servando Santos De La Cruz, a desert wolf dressed in a ranchero's clothes.

When La Avispa first met Servando, she didn't think much of him. Servando was a coffee-brown man with no creamer and much older than La Avispa. He had a fat bulbous nose and a thin graying mustache. His game was played low and slow. Grinding her down and grooming her.

"Monse, you are so beautiful. You remind me of my daughter back in Guanajuato."

Monse never saw him coming, and after three months, he pushed himself on her with the tenacity of an old pimp. In those days, seeing a young teenage girl with an older man was expected. Most of these teenage girls were with bulging bellies before their wedding day. Though Mexico had an age of consent, it was rarely enforced in rural towns.

Servando told La Avisap stories of his land in Guanajuato. He told her he owned a ranch and had a small crew of ranch hands, poor, half-starved Indians he was grateful to overwork. He promised to take La Avispa to his rancho and introduce her to his daughters. La Avispa was twelve then, but she thought herself much older mostly because her mother constantly bragged that La Avispa had developed "un cuerpaso," which had all the men in town sweating. In La Avispa's head, she was already a woman with a cuerpaso and ready to leave her little town. I'm sure her family expected a fine bride-dowery because one thing was certain, her sisters would not fetch a dime.

Servando's consistent grind made La Avispa feel special and wanted. He brought her small decorated combs, paper flowers, and sweet cajeta. His promise of taking her to Guanajuato hooked her. Before she could grasp the gravity of her commitment, she imagined herself dancing in the streets of Guanajuato.

One day, La Avispa's sister, Natty, caught Servando leaning over the counter, brushing La Avispa's hair with one hand while rubbing his penis with the other.

"Pinche animal," Natty yelled at him. "Largate."

Servando let go of his penis, grabbed La Avispa with both hands, and kissed her before running off. La Avispa made Natty promise not to tell their father.

When La Avispa got home, her father called her into the kitchen in a stern voice. His voice echoed like the slap he planted on her for kissing Julio, and the side of her face ached when she heard his voice. She tightly clutched the bright paper flowers and remembered what Servando had told her.

"People are going to test our love." He exhaled into her ear. "They are just jealous because they have never felt a love like this."

Servando's words gave her strength. She walked into that kitchen, ready for war. If her father stood ten feet tall, she would be twenty. He let out a deep exhale and raised his hand to slap her. La Avispa jumped back and pulled open her blouse.

"Look at your daughter now, Papa!" exposing the upper part of her shoulder and arm. Her father squinted to get a good look. Just above the closed crevice of her armpit, where her breast, armpit, and shoulder fold into each other, shined a round purple bruise the size of a mouth.

Her little hickey. Her little secret. For two days,

she had kept the bruise hidden from her sisters by refusing to change in front of them. They thought it odd because they shared the same room and often bathed together. It had been that way since they were babies. But for the past two and a half weeks, La Avispa bathed alone or not at all.

Bam, La Avispa flashed that little hickey at her father. "I'm in love with him," she snarled. "He's going to marry me."

Her father kept his hand cocked, but she kept her blouse open, exposing her little purple badge of courage.

"I know you're in love, Mija." He lowered his arm as if defeated. "Your sisters told me everything." His voice was smooth and paced. Calm. He reached out to hug his daughter. She recoiled, half expecting his affection to be a trap. He motioned for her to step forward. He smiled. His sun-wrinkled face and white mustache made her feel welcomed, like when she was a little girl playing out on the farm, and he would call her over to give her a piece of jamoncillo candy. When La Avispa was a little girl, she would pretend that her father's graying mustache was a pair of angel wings that opened when he laughed. She hugged him so hard she knocked the wind out of him.

"I know, Mija." He patted her head. "If he's to marry you, then we must meet. Surely, he is a man of honor."

She nodded her head, "He is Papa, He is."

"When you see him again, please tell him I'd like

to meet with him."

"Tomorrow, Papa. Tomorrow. He's coming back to the store."

The following day. Servando rode up to the puesto. Servando had a leathery-faced Tarahumara Indian in the passenger side of his truck.

La Avispa almost jumped the counter, trying to get to Servando. She sped past the old lady shopping for Mennonite cheese and dry beans. She ran to Servando, and they embraced. He grabbed her by the back of the neck, tilted her head back, and kissed her. He forced his tongue into her mouth. La Avispa clawed at his chest and then let out a moan. He drove his hips into her hips. She pulled back and placed both her hands on his chest.

"Guess what?"

He nodded at her and kissed her some more.

"I told my Papa about us."

"What?" His eyes opened wide.

"What exactly did you tell Don Luna?

"That you love me, of course. That we're getting married."

He took a few steps back and put his hands up.

"I never said all that."

"But we are, right? I mean, I let you do things to me. That means we're supposed to get married."

"No, it doesn't. Don't be ridiculous. You're still a little girl."

She put her hands to her face to cry. She felt a tap on her shoulder and shrugged it off, thinking it was Servando.

"Mi'ja," said the old woman.

La Avispa turned to her. The old, dark woman raised her right hand and pointed at Servando. "Tein cuidado, Mi'ja." The words flew out of the old woman's mouth, dancing around La Avispa's face like gray moths. The old leathery lady's words had sent a shiver down La Avispa's spine, and she felt the need to look back at her love. She needed to see his soft eyes. She needed to be comforted by his warm smile.

When she turned to look at Servando, she saw her two brothers standing next to him in his truck. They were giants compared to Servando. El Gitano had his arm around Servando like they were old friends about to take a picture. El Gitano leaned in real close to Servando's face. He wants to take a bite out of his face, thought La Avispa. Her brother could go from a loving sibling to a rabid dog in no time.

Her other brother, Yucando, stood at the side of the truck, his shoulder pressed against the door so that the Indian couldn't get out.

La Avispa's sisters had set her up.

Then, like in some spaghetti western, La Avispa's father rode up over the hill on his honey-brown Criollo horse. The sun was setting in the background.

Her father's nostrils were flared, and his eyes were blood red and bulging.

Indio panicked and tried to push the passenger door open, but Yucando leaned into the door. He reached for the driver's door and pulled on the handle. El Gitano tightened his arm around the back of Servando's neck and slammed him against the driver-side door. Servando looked at Indio, but Indio shrugged his shoulder and mouthed the words "Lo siento."

Servando turned to La Avispa. Maybe she could help calm her brother down. But they were stone-cold killers that grew up slaughtering pigs, goats, chickens, and dogs. Blood did not bother her brothers.

La Avispa had no words. She knew better than to interfere with her brothers. They had no problems smacking her or her tattle-tale sisters. So much like Indio in the truck, she, too, shrugged her shoulders.

Her father rode the galloping horse down the hillside. He lashed the horse's back thighs. The horse's nostrils flared as its muscles rippled from above its tight ankles into his chest.

La Avispa's father pulled his 30-30 carbine from the horse's side as he rode up to the truck. He placed the rifle across his lap, leaned down, and slapped Servando clean across the mouth. Of course, Servando's legs went wobbly, but El Gitano held him up.

Lalo pulled the reigns of his horse, and the beautiful Criollo stallion kicked its front legs up and stood on its hind legs before settling down.

"I didn't know she was your daughter."

La Avispa looked at her dad, then back at Servando, and shrugged her shoulders.

Her Father walked to Servando and, without saying a word, crashed the butt of the rifle into Servando's face. The blow dropped Servando to his knees, and blood ran down his forehead.

"Please, don't," Servando sobbed loud and shamefully. "I'll never... I promise."

La Avispa's father gave his rifle to his son, then gave his hand to help Servando up. He pulled Servando to his feet and then punched Servando in the mouth. Servando went limp and fell to the ground. La Avispa's father kicked Servando over and over again.

Servando gushed out blood onto the hot desert dirt.

Lalo looked over at his daughter. "Monserrat! Look at this man. He's a liar with no lands and no cattle. He's a ranch hand, bought and paid for, just like that Indio in the truck."

Her voice choked up, and tears streaked her face. "That's not true."

"Ask him about his wife. Ask him about the girl he left pregnant in Juarez or the one he left in Cualtemipoco."

"That's not true!"

"That Indian in the truck is worth more than this pig shit."

El Gitano, and Yucando, dragged Servando to the back of the truck and tossed him onto the bed. It did not look like Servando was breathing. Yucando smacked the truck's rear like slapping a horse's ass. Indio gave a thumbs up into the rear-view mirror, slid over to the driver's side, turned over the engine, and sped off.

For the next three weeks, La Avispa wandered around aimlessly, a ghost half asleep, lost without love. Her sisters tried to cheer her up. They brought her mazapan and paper flowers, but nothing would snap La Avispa out of her gloom. Her brothers brought her a baby rabbit that they named Gusipi, but she set it loose on the farm, and one of the dogs got a hold of it and tore it apart.

Then one day, as if rising from the dead, Servando returned. Her heart fluttered and jumped wildly in her chest when she saw his beat-up red truck pull up. She pulled her thick black hair back and tied it into a ponytail. Then she pinched her cheeks so they would turn rosy, giving her the appearance of blushing. A trick she had learned from watching her mother.

Servando stepped out of the truck like stepping into a tub with too hot water. He tucked a Colt Model 1917 into the back of his jeans. La Avispa ran to him. He removed his straw cowboy hat, exposing the stitches on his scalp. The stitched skin was puffy and greasy. Both his eyes were black, but only his left eye was swollen.

She hugged him, and he kissed her on the forehead.

"I thought you were dead." She cried.

"Not without you, mi Amor." His hips dug into her.

As she hugged him, she felt the gun tucked in the back of his dungarees. She assured him that her father was out of town, a lie she spun to help ease his tense shoulders.

They agreed to keep their love a secret until he could prove himself. He promised her that he would ask her father for her hand in marriage. But above all else, he lied and told her he coveted her love. He asked to meet behind the grove to prove his love to her.

And for a while, all was good. La Avispa's father thought he had put the fear of God into Servando and that a lying coward like Servando would never return for a piece of naive young ass. But her father did not know his daughter had often met with Servando at the grove. On multiple occasions, they had groped each other while under the protective watchful eye of Indio. He kept a lookout for La Avispa's brothers. Did he sneak a couple of peeks at a topless La Avispa? I suspect so.

She likened herself to Juliet, caught in a hurricane of love so intense that not even death's cold touch could destroy it.

Then one day, La Avispa's sisters overheard La Avispa talking to herself in the mirror.

"Mister and Misses Servando Herndez de la Cruz Delignacio," she whispered. "I love you, mi amor, mi querido." La Avispa leaned over and kissed the mirror.

The sisters looked at each other, eyes wide open. They were excited to tell their father. Lalo stood outside, tending to the horses, when he saw his daughters running through the house, calling for him. La Avispa's sisters were so eager to spill the beans that they could hardly speak in complete sentences. "Avispa. Servando. Grove."

"Slow down, Mijas. Take a deep breath."

They told him everything, including that La Avispa had been sneaking out every night. Of course, they lied, claiming that Servando had impregnated La Avispa and that she had planned to run away. Chela, the oldest sister, told their father --much to the horror of his gentle ears-- that Servando had even given La Avispa the old stink finger.

As La Avispa got ready to sneak out of the house that night, her father and two older brothers loaded their well-oiled carbine .30-30s into the holsters hanging from the muscular hips of their horses. They mounted up and set out for the grove.

Lalo and his sons approached the grove. They strapped themselves to their horse's sides before coming over the hill so that it would appear that the horses were without riders. They had their rifles in hand.

Servando pulled up in the same beat-up truck he was hauled out in. Indio sat in the passenger seat. Servando got out of the truck, then motioned for Indio to get out. Servando handed Indio a knife. "Just in case," Servando said. Indio nodded and went to stand lookout. Servando tucked his colt into his back pocket.

"What do you see, Indio?"

"Some horses grazing, Jefe."

"Okay, ponle ojo."

La Avispa arrived from the west. Her hips swished back and forth as she walked towards Servando. His heart pumped hard, and the blood rushed from the thickness of his skull to his brown weenie. As she walked toward him, he savored every bounce and giggle of her prepubescent jubilant splendor. They hugged, and he pulled her thighs against his as he tried to kiss her. He thumbed at his zipper until the zipper's teeth pulled apart.

She had her eyes closed and was kissing him hard. Servando grabbed her hand. He slid her hand down his chest, past his waist, and onto his engorged penis. She had seen her brothers and Don Luna's, but those were never angry and eying her like Servando's. No, this was different. It was veiny and mad.

He mistook her shock for excitement and tried to pull down her long-flowing skirt. She pulled away, but he held tight to her wrist and kept her hand on his crotch.

"Stop it," shouted La Avispa. "I told you, not again, not till you marry me."

But Servando, deaf and blind with lust, refused

to hear her cries to stop. He pawed at her, licking her lips and moaning. He unbuttoned her blouse and licked at her chest. She cried for him to stop.

"Then why did you bring me here," he shouted.

He pushed her back onto the ground and fell on top of her. She continued to struggle, but he grabbed her wrists with one hand and held them above her head.

When Lalo clicked his rifle hammer back, it echoed throughout the grove. The click of the hammer sounded loud as thunder. Servando, the Tarahumara, and La Avispa all snapped to attention. At that moment, Servando let go of La Avispa's wrists. She scrambled out from under him and buttoned her shirt so fast she missed two buttons.

Servando got to his feet and pulled his Colt. He had no time to put his dick away. He aimed the gun to the right. Nothing but some stupid horses grazing. The Tarumara ran over to Servando.

"Boss, your verguita."

Servando looked down to see himself still exposed.

He hunched over and fumbled with his gun and his zipper.

La Avispa had gotten to her feet and ran towards the hill.

A gunshot boomed, and the Tarahumara fell to the ground, clenching his gut and yelling in pain.

Servando, startled by the boom of Lalo's rifle, dropped his gun. The gun went off as it struck the ground. The bullet whizzed by, grazing El Gitano's horses in the ass. The horse bucked and jumped El Gitano to the ground.

"Que chingao?"

El Gitano cocked his rifle and fired at Servando. The bullet hit Servando's left arm. Servando scrambled to the ground, fumbling with his colt. He fired back, but his rusty Colt misfired.

The other De La Luna men released themselves from their horses and charged at Servando, fidgeting with his gun. When Servando looked up, the three men stood before him, each man aiming his rifle at Servando's chest.

Servando dropped his gun and threw his hands into the air. He called La Avispa, but she didn't answer. She had run away and was too far gone to hear him sobbing.

"Please," Servando begged. The tears rolled down his face.

El Gitano picked up Servando's Colt and tucked it in his waistband.

"You want to fuck my daughter?"

"I have money," Servando cried. "We can arrange something, a courtship, a marriage?"

"Callate, Guey." El Gitano said. Then he walked up and punched Servando in the jaw. The blow knocked

Servando to the floor.

"I love her!" Servando screamed. "I love you, Avispa!" He screamed louder so that she could hear it no matter how far away she had run.

The three men laughed as they squeezed their triggers. The muzzle flashes lit up Servando.

"And that's why you don't mess with La Avispa," Monse said. She smiled at me and poked the side of my belly with her finger. "Or you'll get stung." She laughed when the jab startled me.

I asked her why the horses weren't startled when the rifles when off.

"Didn't you pay attention? They strapped themselves to the sides."

"Yes, but how did they aim so accurately?"

"Don't ask stupid questions, Sharlie." She snapped. "You see, I knew my sisters would tell. Servando was very handsome, pero era Viejo." She laughed.

She turned her back to me and pretended to go to sleep, snoring and everything.

Jesus and I Separate Pepper's Clothes

Three weeks after Pepper's funeral, once things felt calm and we all fell back into the rhythm of life. Jesus and I decided it was time to clear out Pepper's belongings. He had things that none of us wanted or needed, little knick-knack reminders of his life that were headed for the trash. We separated Pepper's clothes into three piles, clothes to donate and sell. We didn't keep much of Pepper's clothes because Jesus was too fat to fit into them. I can still pull off some of Pepper's clothes. I'm not as doughy as Jesus. So I decided to keep Pepper's gray suit, his bolo tie, and a couple of his pearl-buttoned cowboy shirts. Jesus wanted Pepper's orange ostrich-skin cowboy boots, even though they were a size eight and a half.

"Dude, how are you going to get those big ass lonches of yours into Pepper's boots?" I pointed to his size eleven wide as a meatloaf foot.

But Jesus doesn't answer. Instead, he throws up his middle finger. And laughs. "I'm taking his hat too."

"If your feet can't fit into the boots, what makes you think your fat head will fit into his hat."

We both laugh.

The plan was to load Jesus's truck with the furniture and then call Goodwill to pick up the bags of clothes lying on the sidewalk. I wonder if those who buy Pepper's coats will dress them up with a turquoise and silver horse head lapel pin. Will the new owner smell like anise and cinnamon, have mahogany skin, be bald, and flash a silver incisor when they smile? What will happen to Pepper's polyester slacks and cowboy shirts with pearl-inlay buttons? What happens to the things we value while living? Do they end up in the landfill among used diapers and broken plates?

When I separated Pepper's mattress from the box spring, several flesh-colored rubber bands fell from the underside of the mattress. I grabbed the thickest rubber band and tried to make a ponytail from my scraggly mullet.

"What the fuck, man?" Jesus laughed and pointed at me. "Calmala Van Halen, your hair ain't long enough. You look like a bull dyke."

"Fuck off."

"Those are Pepper's rubber bands, dummy. He used them to choke his chile." Jesus makes the international sign for masturbation.

I laughed as I pulled the rubber band from my hair. I held it up to the light. Several greasy strands dangled and glistened on the hoop of the rubber band.

"He might need this."

I take the rubber band into the living room, where Monse sits on the couch crying.

"Sharlie, what are you doing with that?" she asks.

"Thought the Viejo could use it," I say. I walk to the entertainment center, which houses a leather box filled with Pepper's ashes.

I stand at the glass door of the entertainment center and see myself between photos of my grandfather and a picture of Henry Vaquero. This marine had served in the Middle East. Henry was the son of Elvia, Monse's friend, and every night during the Iraq War, Monse prayed to the photo of Henry. She'd pray for hours, and all the while, the news of the war would be in the background. I guess her prayers worked because Henry came back unscathed. He died two years later in a motorcycle accident. A car clipped him on the freeway. His motorcycle spun out and slammed Henry into the concrete divider, splitting his head open. Though Henry had died, his mother, Elvia, claimed that Monse's prayers were the only reason her son had returned home safe from the war in the Middle East.

In the photo of Pepper, Pepper poses at three-quarters of a profile, and the background and photographer's lights cast a soft halo around Pepper's head. Henry Vaquero is dressed in his Marine formals, including the white hat with the Marine emblem, a gold eagle holding an anchor over the world. Henry is all smiles.

For a moment, I thought about removing Henry's photo, I mean, the guy isn't even family, and here we have him on the same shelf as Pepper. Besides, Pepper never liked Henry. Hell, Pepper never liked anybody.

I opened the glass door and laid the rubber bands

on the leather box holding Pepper's ashes. I got lost in the grain texture of the leather box. It reminded me of Pepper's thick chestnut brown fingers. I thought about his meaty palms and the thick callous that bordered his fingers. The residue of hard labor.

Jesus came up from behind.

"Don't be getting all emotional, Pussy. We still have a lot of shit to move." He punched my shoulder.

Even though I wasn't crying, I wiped my eyes just in case. I didn't want Jesus to give me a hard time, at least not more than usual. "I'm not getting emotional, Puto. I was just wondering why Monse keeps this picture of some asshole who isn't part of the family."

"You know how she is. She likes to linger with the dead."

After clearing out Pepper's belongings, we sat silently at the kitchen table. Monse served us spaghetti noodles slathered in sour cream and cheese. I ask her what she wants to do with Pepper's room.

"I don't know," she says. "But I wish I could seal up the bathroom so I never have to see where Pepper died."

"Don't be ridiculous," Jesus said.

"You don't be ridiculous, Baboso," Monse snapped back. "With your chiqi verga and your puta wife."

Not much was said after that exchange.

Jesus left as soon as he was done wolfing down his spaghetti. It's a shame because he promised me a ride if I helped him load the furniture. He didn't even say goodbye. I knew something was up when he didn't get seconds of the spaghetti, which is rare for Jesus.

After Jesus left, Monse cried out for Pepper. When she looked up at me, her eyes swollen and red from the crying, and asked me if I would spend the night. She doesn't want to be alone.

"I can still hear Pepper struggling on the bathroom floor."

I tell her I have to work in the morning. I tell her I have to catch the bus. Anything to get out from under the weight and tension in Monse's house. I wanted to go home. I wanted to drink quarts and quarts of beer. I wanted to roll a joint, sit on my couch and listen to Jim Morrison wail away as the Doors pump out the blues. Most of all, I wanted to be away from Monse and the gravity of her sorrow.

On the way out, Monse traced the sign of the cross on my forehead. Her blessing and a mumbled prayer chilled my spine. I shook to get rid of the sensation.

I stopped at the pile of clothes on the curb and rummaged through the bag. It didn't feel right to toss Pepper's clothes out like trash. He took pride in how he looked and took care of his clothes. He would've never allowed his clothes to sit on a curb, waiting to be picked up like a working girl on Dyer.

I pulled some pants and cowboy shirts out of the bags. I tried Pepper's shirt on. It fits tight around my gut, but maybe I can stretch it.

I didn't speak to Monse for a couple of weeks.

"Estoy tan solita," she said over the phone. "I don't know if I can last."

I don't want to hear it. I'm happy in this world where my only concern is my two hundred seventy-five-dollar rent for my attic apartment and getting Julie back. I didn't want to get pulled into Monse's world of loneliness. I felt like my apartment was shrinking in on me. Her guilt grasped onto my heart, and she won't let go. Not ever.

"I have to go. I'm late for work," I lie.

"Please, Sharlie," she says. "I just want to talk to somebody. Let me tell you a story, like when you were a kid?"

I sank deeper and deeper into Monse's gravity. It pulled me down and stretched me thin with thoughts of Julie and some greasy waiter.

I promised Monse I would visit her as soon as I could get some time off. I didn't have to go to work for the next two days.

El Gitano

Not all of my Grandmother's stories were fiction. Not all of her stories were about vampire donkeys. Sometimes she talked about living on the rancho in Mexico, where she sheered lambs, made cheese, and took in the Chihuahua desert's rich blue, orange, and teal sunsets.

I imagined her brothers were these tall, wide-shouldered vaqueros with tough leathery necks and thick heavy hands. They were the type of men that wrestled steer, planted crops into the earth, that lived with the sun on their backs. They lived and worked from dawn till dusk. They could outwork the sun.

Growing up, I measured myself against them. Monse's father and brothers were the standard, the primal measure of my manliness. I had to be tough because they were tough. I had to work hard because they worked hard. They were honest, so I was honest, or at least I thought myself to be honest. As I got older, I saw the flaws. Perhaps that's what made them heroes to me. They had all been killed.

To hear my grandmother talk about her brothers was like hearing a devotee talk about their religion. For Monse, her brothers were fearless men cut from wood and stone that she crafted out of language and memory. El Gitano, Guagiro, and Yucando were Monse's pride. Hearing stories about them was my link to Mexico, where we were once kings.

My grandmother would never admit this, but she loved El Gitano, the oldest of the three, above her other brothers. Or at least she told more stories about him than anybody else. El Gitano had long, curly hair and smelled like anise and sandel wood. He stood a foot above any other Mexican in Aldama and was said to be so handsome that every woman secretly desired him.

I never got a chance to meet El Gitano. He had died long before my time. However, when Monse spoke of him, her eyes lit up, and a giant smile crossed her face.

Remembering back, I was a soft-bellied ten-year-old boy when it occurred to me to ask Monse how El Gitano had died. I wasn't slow to the question. I wanted to ask her how he died since I was eight. That was the first time I saw something die. My friend, Francis Leva, killed a cat by holding it down and stuffing a pair of firecrackers up its ass.

Leva had caught the cat by leaving a can of tuna in the alley. This calico walked over, licking its chops, ready to get at that tuna. You could tell this cat ran the alley because all the other cats backed off. The calico came strutting, looked around, and dug its head into the can. That's when Francis pounced on the cat. He threw a blanket over the cat and dropped all his weight onto the cat. The cat yelped under the heavy blanket as Leva wrestled it down.

Once Leva had it in position, with the cat's hindquarters exposed, he called me over. I popped out from behind the fence. Leva held two firecrackers up in the air.

"Bring the lighter, Charlie."

He forced the first firecracker into the cat's puckered rear. The cat screamed horrible yells. Leva had tied the firecrackers, so one cuete dangled from the cat's ass. I ran over and handed him the lighter. Honestly, I didn't want to do it, but Leva was my only friend, so I pulled out his dad's lighter and lit the fuse. Leva jumped off the cat, and the cat bolted out of the alley and towards the ditch. We tried to follow, but the cat moved too fast.

At first, we heard a muffled explosion, then the sound of the second Black Cat blasted through the air. Leva laughed a big bucked-tooth laugh. Can't say I didn't laugh too.

Then I heard the cat's deep moaning of pain.

"Let's go kill it," Leva said.

He ran into the house and returned with a tennis racket and a peewee-league Jose Canseco baseball bat. He handed me the bat, smiled, and motioned to jump the fence and follow the noise. The cat's moans grew louder and louder. My heart was pumping faster and faster. Sweat gathered between my palm and the bat. I didn't want to kill that poor animal, but I didn't want to lose a friend, either.

We found the cat two houses away. The poor thing limped and cried, meowing these blood-curdling meows. A trail of blood leaking from its blown-out anus.

"Do it, Charlie!" Leva said. I could hear the excitement in his voice. "Do it, mijo!"

He pointed to the bat in my hand.

"Fuck no," I said.

I dropped the bat and backed away.

Leva picked up the Jose Canseco bat and raised it up into the air. He gave me a toothy smile and brought that bat onto the cat's back. The cat screamed and collapsed. Leva swung again and again and again until the cat's cry was replaced by the wet thud of the bat hitting the smear that had been the cat. He turned to me and laughed, then he took a final swing.

It all happened too fast. I ran away, back to Leva's house. I wanted to tell his Mom, but that would make me a tattle-tail, and I couldn't risk the stigma.

"Where are you going, Charlie?" I could hear Leva yelling. "Don't be such a pussy."

That night, after I showered, I asked her, "Ma, come se murió tu Hermano, El Gitano?"

She looked at me and pressed her forehead into my cheek.

"I thought I had told you how."

"No," I said. "You never have."

She looked at me for a second. I felt nervous. Maybe I had asked for something that I shouldn't have. For a moment, I thought about that cat and Leva's stupid face, smiling as he swung his bat.

Then Monse whispered, "It all started with this little black goat I had named Cheva." Monse extended the *Ch* sound until it tickled me to my butt.

"Cheva had this huge belly that extended almost to the floor and long swollen utters." Monse paused for a second as if contemplating some profound idea. "Esta embarazada." She looked at me, gauging my reaction.

"Then, early one August morning, before the sun had risen, I heard a cry rip through the house, waking the entire family. It reminded me of the awful sound pigs make when they are rounded up for slaughter. I ran into the kitchen where my brothers and my father were standing.

'Go back to bed, Chiquita,' my father commanded.

'Que es eso?' I grabbed my father's leg as the screech stormed through the house.

'Un lobo,' said El Gitano as he loaded our grandfather's Carbine 30-30. 'Y lo voy a matar,' he snarled.

El Gitano opened the back door and inched his way toward the barn. His rifle cocked and pressed against his right shoulder. We followed behind as he moved, careful not to make any noise. I ran up behind him and grabbed his leg. He nudged me away and nodded for me to go back inside. I shook my head no. Then he puckered his lips and motioned for me to be quiet. I followed behind him, taking care not to make a noise. The screams were getting heavy in the cool morning air. On the horizon, the night sky's darkness had broken like a fever, and the approaching daylight made the stars sparkle as I had never seen them before or since.

We stood at the barn's entrance. El Gitano's breathing slowed to a deep, steady rhythm. The cries had stopped but were replaced by growls and the gnawing sound of a beast wrestling something away with its jaws. I peeked through the crack where the barn gate hinges and saw the gray desert wolf's amber and golden eyes lock with mine. The brown and gray fur on his snout was matted with blood. The wolf snarled, exposing his yellow fangs. Then bang. The rifle recoiled. The flash from the rifle barrel lit up the room, and I saw my Cheva on the floor. Her big black eyes looked up at me. Her breathing was steady but labored. Her tongue was hanging from her mouth. The wolf had torn her neck."

Monse closed her eyes, and I thought she might be imitating the goat because her breathing had become unsteady and somewhat labored. Then I realized that she had drifted to sleep. Her memories guided her dream, and she cried out, lost between her dream and waking life.

"Lo mató, lo mató, lo mató," Monse said with tears running down her face. "Mataron Cheva! Mataron Cheva! Mataron El Gitano!"

I stayed quiet, almost holding my breath for fear that my breathing might snap her out of her dream, that she might come crashing back to reality. I turned around to hug her. She didn't wake.

"Are you okay, Mama?"

Her sobs deepened.

Then Monse's voice changed. It grew gruff and deep. Her body tensed like a rope being pulled taught. And I swear a shadow cast upon her face that exaggerated her features, making her chin look wide and her cheeks sharp. "Oye, Avispa, que rica tu cabra." She said in a deep low tone.

"Por que hermano, por que mataste a mi Cheva?" Monse winced and cried out in her normal voice.

Her voice went back to deep and gruff. "Misericordia, Hermana. Ya estaba hasta la chingada"

"Pero por que tacos? Hermano. Tacos de mi Chiva." She cried.

"Pos que pues hermana, teniamos hambre, tenemos que comer." Monse was sobbing. "No! No!No!"

I nudged her hard with my elbow. "Ma, wake up!"

She sat up, startled. "What! What! What! Guey?"

She took a deep breath, then lay back on her pillow.

"What was I talking about?"

"You were about to tell me how El Gitano died."

She nodded twice, "It all started con tu pinche Abuelo. Pepper siempre se puso hasta la madre con ese pinche veneno." she said. "And that's how El Gitano started drinking because of Pepper. That's how I met your Abuelo. One day, some scrawny Indio Apache-looking guy showed up at our doorstep, asking for work. And my brother, El Gitano, had mercy on him. Turns out that feo indo became your grandfather."

"What about your goat?" I asked. "Didn't he..."

"You see, Charlie," she interrupted. "El Gitano was no coward. People put respect on his name. He would flap up some dust with their lips if they didn't. If a woman across the street gave him the evil eye, he would go punch her eye out. Once, a neighborhood dog barked at him, and El Gitano gutted the dog with a hatchet. If any man stood up to El Gitano, El Gitano would slap the piss out of them and then kill them. He had huevos, Mijo. Not like you, you're still soft, but soon you too will learn." She poked my soft belly with her middle finger.

"What happened to him, Mama?"

"Let me tell you," she said.

Her eyes glossed over. "It seemed as if the entire town of Aldama was celebrating Alan and Cindy's wedding at the town square. The mariachis strummed their big ole guitars while Folklorico dancers twirled and spun their bright yellow dresses. Marigolds hung in long beautiful strands from the center of the town square across to the very edge of Aldama. All of my family was at that wedding. My brothers, sisters, cousins, and nieces danced in swirls, circles, and curtsies.

At first, Pepper and I sat in the back, near the fountain, because he had some misunderstanding with the bride's brother, Aldama's police captain, Figaro Garcia. I figured it would be best to stay out of Figaro's sight.

Pepper downed a couple of copas of Mezcal, and we had a few beers. I never drink, Charlie, but I had one beer that night. Pepper got nice and loose, and so did I. Then El Gitano shows up and pulled us to the dance floor.

Pepper grabbed my hand and twirled me around the dance floor. He moved in long graceful arches around me, his face dead serious with concentration. Pepper loved dancing but never did it sober. In fact, he never did much sober in those days.

He twirled me around the dance floor, all proud to have me. La Avispa was twisted around by this Indio-Mexicano as dark as a pecan tree.

I didn't feel much like dancing then. I never really liked doing it. But I have to admit, it was a dream watching Pepper dance. I'm not sure how to explain it. He danced rhythmically, sliding around and stomping like a beautiful ritual.

He loved grabbing me by the waist and pulling me to his hips. His callused fingers roughed up my tender hands. We danced in extended sweeping circles. Pepper was getting lighter on his feet while I stumbled around, trying to keep up. We danced for what felt like hours --sweat pouring down his shirt as he moved and jived his hips. Then the world became dizzy, and I asked Pepper if he could walk me back to our table. But Pepper didn't want to stop. He tried to outlast every person on that dance floor, so he sat me down at the table nearest him, the captain's table. He returned to the dance floor. One of the mariachis brought a hat over to Pepper and laid it at Pepper's feet.

'Braulio! Braulio!' they all chanted.

Pepper clasped his hands behind his back, then he bowed. The music stopped for half a second. Pepper puffed his chest out and tapped the toe of his boot three times. The trumpet player blasted his horn, and the rest of the band followed with a zapateado. Pepper danced around the hat, shuffling, skipping, and pounding to the beat. Almost like a tap dancer, but more Mexican. When the song finished, everybody clapped and cheered. Pepper smiled his big mustached smile, and then he took a bow.

We returned to our table, and Pepper took a deep swig from his bottle. He coughed, grabbing at his throat, but he kept at it and took another swig like he had a vendetta against that fucking bottle, and one way or another, he needed to finish it. We made it out to the dance floor a few more times. But then Pepper started complaining, 'The world is spinning too fast, Vieja.'

I urged him to sit down, but he got angry and spun around, bumping into the other dancers.

And then that pendejo messed up. You see, in all Pepper's joy and dance, he made the mistake of smashing into the police captain and his wife. Pepper had stomped all over her dress.

'Hey, pendejo,' the captain said.

'Vales verga, guey,' Pepper said.

The captain reached for his pistol, but his wife stopped him. 'Me la vas a pagar, Braulio,' said the captain before slapping Pepper. The smack was drowned out by the band. No one saw the commotion; if they did, they did not stop dancing, singing, and celebrating. The captain had built a reputation for smacking around drunks but never arresting them. I sent Pepper back to the table. I figured I could keep an eye on him till he cooled down. I kept an eye on the Captain too.

Pepper sat there, mad and drunk, a red handprint on his dark cheek. He wanted retaliation. I saw it in his eyes. I knew he wanted to take his pistol out, but that would only get him killed. Instead, he sat red-faced and cross-eyed, feeling the gun's weight against his ankle.

Things cooled, and everybody was celebrating, including Pepper, who had moved on to beer. When the bride cut the cake, Pepper took the opportunity to sneak around the fountain and take a long piss. He unzipped his zipper, then let the hot stream of urine flow into the fountain.

'Que chingados estas haciendo?' the police captain yelled behind Pepper.

Pepper squeezed his but cheeks and spun around. The Captain had his right hand on his military gun.

'Nothing,' mumbled Pepper.

'Pinche Braulio, no te la vas ha acabar.'

Pepper jumped off the lip of the fountain and ran back to the party. I'm sure the entire crowd was a blur to Pepper. Maybe El Gitano was the only face he recognized, so Pepper ran to him to explain what had happened.

El Gitano and Pepper marched back to the fountain. The captain had his gun drawn, waiting for Pepper to come back. But when the captain saw El Gitano, he froze.

'Hey, Figaro!' El Gitano said. 'Did you slap my cuñado?'

'He trampled all over my wife, then pissed in the fountain.'

El Gitano towered over the Captain.

'Holster your gun,' El Gitano growled.

The Captain trembled and twitched as he holstered his gun. The Captain clicked the button of the leather holster and was about to say something when El Gitano slapped the Captain across the face so hard the Captain went stiff as a corpse. His head hit the saltillo-tiled floor, and the Captain was out.

Pepper kicked the captain twice in the ass before taking the captain's gun and tucking it in his waistband.

'You were scared of this guy?' El Gitano asked.

'Watch this, guey.'

Pepper unzipped his pants, stood over the Captain, and then let out a long warm stream of piss onto the Captain's back. El Gitano followed and also pissed on the Captain. They laughed as the hot liquor piss splattered over the captain's uniform."

Monse looked down at me, checking to see if I had fallen asleep. My eyes were wide open at the thought of my grandfather being so drunk. The idea of my grandfather dancing and pissing on the captain was beyond anything I had ever seen from him. Not my sweet Grandfather. My Grandfather prayed at dawn and never took a sip of alcohol.

"A few weeks later, while El Gitano sat at a bar, the Police Captain walked in and shot my brother in the back," Monse said. "The Captain was a coward who could never beat El Gitano, even at his best. So like all cowards, he attacked my brother from behind." She looked back down at me and ran her hand through my curly hair, which reminded her of El Gitano. "Now go to sleep, you little putillo." She laughed, put her heavy arm around me, closed her eyes, and went straight to sleep, snoring deep into my ear.

I stayed up that night, staring at the little bumps of the popcorn ceiling. I wanted her to continue. I wanted to know what happened after the Captain shot El Gitano. I knew there was more to the story, so I let my mind cruise the landscape of the town of Aldama until I saw the Police Captain lying face down near the fountain.

The Captain woke up after the party ended. He stammered around the town square, confused about why he smelled like dog piss and beer. His head hurt, but he managed through the pain. We walked out of the town square and into the streets towards his home. He wondered why his wife hadn't gone looking for him, why she had left him there on the floor. He pulled off his stinking jacket, took a whiff of it, then pulled away in disgust.

When he got home, the front door felt heavier than he had remembered. He used the whole of his body weight to open the door. The house felt humid, and he caught an unfamiliar smell. He heard a sound. The pig grunts his wife would make when they were having sex. He reached for his military pistol as he ran to his bedroom door. No luck.

The Captain charged in, holding his hand out like holding a gun. His wife was on her hands and knees. El Gitano was behind her, pumping at a fevered pace.

"Figaro!" Shouted the Captain's wife. "Close the fucking door!"

The Captain's eyes blurred. He wouldn't cry in front of his wife or El Gitano.

El Gitano looked at the Captain, "She said to close the fucking door."

The Captain closed the door, went to the kitchen

table, and sat down. Tears welled up and ran down his cheeks. He had known about El Gitano and his wife. Maybe the entire town knew about his wife. But tonight, he could no longer deny what he had to do.

He had lost his gun somewhere between the town square and his house. He looked around the kitchen for anything he could use. Then he saw the meat cleaver on the kitchen counter that he had used to spatchcock chickens and cut through the pork rib meat. He had used that cleaver thousands of times, and when he picked it up from the kitchen counter, it felt lighter than ever. His hand fit perfectly around the cleaver's wooden handle. He held the blade up to his face and marveled at the jagged edge, which he had sharpened time and time again. He heard his wife moaning from the other room. He spat on the blade, rushed down the hallway, and quietly opened the door. He crept up behind El Gitano, who was too busy and drunk to notice the Captain.

The Captain raised the cleaver and swung it down, striking El Gitano between his neck and shoulder. El Gitano screamed "Que chingados!"

The Captain pulled the cleaver from El Gitano's neck. Blood splattered onto the Captain's wife's back. She, too, screamed out. El Gitano grabbed his neck to slow the bleeding, but the cleaver had cut deep into his carotid artery.

El Gitano grabbed the Captain by the neck, but the Captain swung again, deep into El Gitano's rib meat. The Captain hacked away at El Gitano, turning him to pulp. Then the Captain turned to his wife, I love you, Corazon, then he raised the cleaver into the air and split her skull.

And that's how and why the Captain killed El Gitano.

The Payton Meats

Pepper was in the middle of prayer when the Payton Meat Company called. He had worked as a Brazero for years, picking cotton and chile. The backbreaking labor had him wanting to go back to Mexico. Then Payton called, and with that call came a chance to earn real money.

The morning of the interview, he waxed his boots and imagined how good it would feel when he left his current job. The Brazeros program had almost broken him. Working those fields in the desert had dried him into a beef jerky of a man. The unforgiving west Texas sun had turned his hands into wood, rough from picking. Despite the hard work and brutal sun, Pepper kept a smile on his face and eventually made good friends with the other Brazeros.

The Brazeros program ensured his naturalization, but he didn't cross the Rio Grande to live in poverty. His manifest destiny was not to go west but to cross north. Go north, my son, to the land of milk, honey, and güeras.

During his Brazero days, he had so much momentum he could go through a brick wall. He felt like a machine, like a workhorse, and by tomorrow, God willing, he would be working at the Payton meat factory.

Pepper woke up at four in the morning. He spent all of the dawn going over interview questions in his head. "Yes, sir, I'm a real hard worker." He said, in a thick Chihuahua accent.

Careful not to roll your R's, he thought.

After an hour of practicing his English, he got dressed. He parted his hair to the right and waxed his mustache with a cedar-scented wax. His wranglers fit snug around his boots but loose around his bum. His skinny hips and no butt made wearing pants without a belt impossible. A feeling of pride washed over him as he cinched his waist with his brown leather belt with a white Aztec calendar stitched onto the buckle. He felt things were turning for the good for the first time since his brother's death. God had answered his prayers; perhaps this was absolution. He opened his medicine cabinet, uncoiled a light blue plastic rosary, then kissed the rosary three times, one for the father, the son, and the holy ghost. Then he folded the rosary and put it back into the medicine cabinet.

His wife, Monse, had all four burners working on the stove. She had Pepper's breakfast cooking in two pans, and in another pan, she had his lunch cooking. The fourth burner had a comal and a flour tortilla puffing with steam.

Her chest swelled at the possibility of having confidence in Pepper again. Since moving to the United States, his drinking and need to cheat on her worsened. Two nights ago, he came home with a prostitute. Monse almost stabbed her to death.

Monse focused her energy on the positive. She no longer loved him but would tolerate him on some level.

He's getting a good job. She repeated to herself over and over again. In those morning hours, it became her mantra. *He's getting a good job, he's getting a good job, he's getting a good job.* Those words became a fever pitch burning up her doubt.

Jesus sat eager and excited to taste whatever lard-fried breakfast Monse had cooked. Monse made eggs and chorizo, beans, and less his sense of smell was mistaken, she had fried up some bologna too. Jesus sipped his father's coffee while waiting for the food. He liked sipping from his dad's mug. It made him feel proud like he was gaining his dad's strength with every sip. He saw himself as being as strong and hard-working as his father. *Every hard-working man needs his coffee*, Jesus thought.

The room was filled with the beautiful scent of chorizo and beans frying in Snow Cap lard. Monse dropped two scoops of beans into the skillet and mashed them with a wooden spoon. Squeezing the life out of them. The beans emaciated into a thick swirl of chorizo and legumes. Hot lard and bean juice splashed against her forearm, burning her and knocking her out of her trance. The image of Pepper and that prostitute in the living room flashed before her. She struggled to find her mantra again. Her mind had gone blank of all language. She tried to speak but could only see that prostitute's fat round face moving up and down.

She heard the neighbor's children running upstairs, jumping off furniture, and stomping.

"Hijo de su puta madre." Her words came crashing back.

Her mind snapped to the idea that her family had to leave Segundo Barrio. *Dear God, Pepper needs this job. Por favor, Dios.*

One of the boys upstairs must have fallen because a loud thud boomed through the room, followed by a shrill cry. She wondered how often the neighbors had listened in on her and Pepper. Did her neighbors hear the fighting? Had they heard when Pepper slapped her after a night of heavy drinking? Could they hear her crying? She wondered if they listened in on nights when he came home too drunk to see straight, acting bullish, and needing a place to put his dick. Why didn't they help? Why didn't they call the police when they heard her crying and Pepper raping her? Did they hear the night she jammed a screwdriver into the prostitute's back?

He's getting a good job, she repeated. *He's getting a good job. He's getting a good job.*

When the beans were cooked to a thick brown salty paste, and the chorizo and egg had turned fluffy and red, she turned off the stove, and a broad smile came across her face. She nodded yes a few times as if she had been talking to someone in the room. Then she served her Son and Husband their plates.

Pepper walked into the kitchen, expecting a compliment. Something nice from Monse would have gone a long way for his ego. But she had her back to him, hunched over the stove. Her face was wet from sweat and hot steam. Pepper crept up from behind, slid his hands under her arms, then reached up and squeezed her chichi's. The pain snapped her out of her mantra and back to the all too small kitchen.

"Presta esas chichotas," he said, licking his lips like a cartoon wolf.

She jabbed him with her elbow, but he didn't stop.

"Yah! Yah, Guey!"

Suppose Pepper hadn't been in such a good mood. In that case, he might have smacked her upside the head or, at the very least, cussed her out, *pinche Vieja, culera*, but his excitement over a new job kept him in good spirits. Instead, he pinched her nipple hard, then backed away. Jesus was already eating and pretending not to notice.

As a Brazero, Pepper had worked cotton, chili, and pecan seasons. He worked at a farm in Ruidoso during the off-season, tending to racehorses. Pepper had worked the land in some form or another for most of his life. Even though small framed and only five seven, his palms were hard like mahogany, and his nails were thick and white like seashells. His handshake intimidated most soft-palmed men. Puñetas, as he called them. Pepper swore that nobody could outwork him. He knew this, and so did Monse, though she would never admit it.

The interview took place in a trailer outfitted to be an office. The trailer had air-conditioning, which helped cool a sweaty Pepper and the other two prospects in the office. Pepper had recognized the other two men from the Brazeros migrant worker program. He felt confident that he would be hired over them.

The G.M., Gary Fieldmen, a pink balding man with sausage fingers and a blue clip-on tie, sat across from the three men. Gary took deep breaths as if trying to catch his breath after running. Each word seemed to puff and wheeze out of his mouth. Sweat beaded across his gray scalp.

"You all will be working the first shift," puffed Gary. "Starts at five and goes till three. Pays $2.25 plus time and a half overtime." Gary wheezed. "Comprende? Overtime?"

The three men grin and nod.

Gary leaned into his chair and rested his hands on his stomach. "If you have trouble filling out your paperwork, take it to Mary. She'll get you situated," he wheezed. "She's at reception."

Gary stood up, pushed his bulbous stomach into his desk, and extended his hand toward the three men, shaking each of their hands. "Gentlemen, welcome to the Payton Meat Company." He puffed.

The three men stood outside of the trailer, looking at their paperwork. Pepper could speak English, and he did it with an accent that gave him a charm rarely found in a border town. But Pepper's broken English fell short when understanding the legal jargon of an employment contract. Nor had he ever heard the word "receptionist."

And for a brief second, a growing fear in Pepper's stomach crawled up from his gut and into his skull, forming a harsh and nasty idea. *Perhaps he lacked the fortitude and intelligence to work as anything other than a field worker.*

As Pepper looked over to the other two men, he realized they had no idea what to do next or how to read English.

They looked up at Pepper and nodded.

"Braulio Cantero," Pepper said confidently, hiding that little fear monster running around in his head.

"Mucho gusto," said the first squat man. "Renaldo."

"Juan Carlo," said the other man.

All three looked down at their papers. Renaldo shrugged, and Juan Calo let out an almost inaudible wheezy sigh.

Pepper rubbed his tan fingers through his mustache and concluded he would lead these men. What if he helped them get settled in? Then they would forever owe him one. So with the confidence of a civil rights leader, he waived them into the direction of the factory and began his march into his new future. *Besides, if I mess up, I can always blame one of these lame, no English-speaking Sureños.*

The three men marched toward the factory, where they could hear the sound of saws ripping through the meat and bones of some desperate cow carcass.

Much to Pepper's relief, when the three men entered the factory, they were greeted by a large desk and a smiling receptionist. The entrance had the pungent smell of raw meat and fresh animal fat. Pepper had worked at a slaughterhouse in Mexico, and he knew that smell too well.

Pepper flashed a big toothy smile at the receptionist, and she smiled back. Her curly bleached hair bounced past her shoulders and rested on her yellow blouse. Juan Carlo and Renaldo shied behind Pepper as he led them to her desk.

"Can I help you?"

"Yes," said Pepper. "Do you speaky Spanish?"

"You all the new hires?" Her words sank in a long Southern drawl.

The men all nodded in unison. Pepper looked over at the other two and realized they didn't understand a single word from the receptionist's mouth.

"Let me see your Papers."

The three men placed the papers on the desk. She pointed to a line at the bottom of the first page.

"Write your name here and here." Her nails were painted teal, and her perfume cut through the mean smell of decay that filled the rest of the reception area and factory floor.

"This line is your address."

Pepper was getting all kinds of hot standing over her.

"I like your shirt," he said.

The two men pressed forward like they were heavy on his words. Pepper put his hand behind his back and waved the two men to hang back. "I have a car the same color."

He smiled at her. "It's a Maverick."

And, according to Pepper, she blushed.

Though all three men stared at her like she was dinner, Pepper was the only one who spoke English. The other two men never stood a chance.

"Want to see it," Pepper said. His English got more robust with each interaction.

"If you don't have a social security number, leave it blank." She pointed at the paper in front of her.

The double-wide doors to the left of the front desk opened. A man wearing a blood-stained-smock and carrying a thermos that Pepper initially thought to be a hatchet but turned out to be a silver thermos walked through the slitted plastic curtain. A white paper hat covered his head, but parts of his fro stuck out from the sides of the hat. Renaldo and Juan Carlo had never seen a black man, and they were taken aback by his height, broad shoulders, and mahogany skin.

"Hey, Mary." He smiled.

"Williams," she smiled back.

Juan Calo elbowed Pepper. "She must like Negros, huh."

"These the new hires?" Williams interrupted.

Williams, for seventeen years, ever since he was first stationed at Fort Bliss, had heard that same joke hundreds of times over.

"Just getting them situated," Mary said. She handed the papers to Pepper. "Make sure you're here before five. The foreman doesn't mess around when it comes to getting to work late."

"No work today?" Pepper asked.

The two weeks of no pay and inaction had Pepper anxious and frustrated. Without a hard day's work, it was impossible to get a decent sleep. He needed the sweat on his brow, a sore back, heavy legs, and roughed-up hands. For those two weeks, he tortured Monse and his son Jesus. One night, Jesus spilled a cup of water, and Pepper planted a smack across Jesus's face. Or when Monse burned the tortilla, he cussed her out and promised to knock out her front teeth if she ever ruined what little food they had left in the house. He called her a dumb cow.

"Tomorrow," Mary said. "Be here at five."

"Cinco," Williams said. He held his hand up, showing his five fingers.

Pepper stopped at a park bench and ate the bean

torta Monse had made for him. He watched as the alligators in the town square moved in a tight, slow circle and snapped at the birds drinking from the pond.

Pepper arrived at the Payton Meat Factory the following day at four thirty-two. The three-and-a-half-mile walk from his apartment to Payton invigorated his senses, which he needed in the cool dark hours before sunset. On his walk to Payton, he could smell the cold dew pooled on the leaves of the desert flora growing between the cracks of the sidewalks in south-side El Paso's industrial district. As Pepper picked up his pace, the factories along the way lit up as the crews began to arrive and turn over the machine engines that would be used to cut through garments, cardboard, and leather. He carried a brown paper-bag lunch consisting of an avocado torta, an orange, and a bean burrito. The thermos of coffee was folded into his jacket to keep him warm. He ate his bean burrito and drank most of the dark brown bitter coffee while walking to his new job at the Payton Meat Factory. He had never felt prouder.

By the time he got to the factory, his heartbeat was loud and fast. He was awake. He was ready to work, hungry for a new future, hungry to leave the past behind.

He thought Mary would be at her desk, but the desk was empty, and the light was off. He walked past the desk and into the double-wide doors that swallowed him whole and spat him onto the factory floor. The factory's cold refrigerated air surprised Pepper, and he wished he still had a full thermos to keep him warm.

Groups of white-smocked men pushed brooms around the table saws. The men worked fast, and despite the cold, the entire factory floor came to life with the sound of band saws and an occasional blaring horn.

Four men worked each station, one man loading a carcass, another pushing it through, while the third man received it. The fourth man would place the meat into separate bins. The fourth man raised his hand when the containers were full, and two other men would bring an empty cart. They were human ants moving in unison to the symphony of the Payton Meat plant.

Pepper walked along the perimeter of the factory floor, watching the men work. Most were Mexican and had stern leathery faces and tired eyes. Among the workers was a short round man with a clipboard, inspecting the stations and nodding in approval of the other men. When he spotted Pepper, he sighed and walked right over to Pepper.

"Can I help you?"

"Yes, you speaky Spanish?"

"Little bit," said the man. "You the new hire? " The man looked at the watch stretched over his thick hairy wrist. "You're temprano. I like that."

Pepper introduced himself and shook the beefy hand of the foreman, Mister Abdul. Abdul explained how the cutting room floor operated, but Pepper could not hear over the saws cutting bone. After the facility tour, Abdul led Pepper into the back to the employee locker room.

"Remember, Braulio," Abdul explained, "The good meat goes to the butchers. The rest goes to our links department, where it's made into hot dogs, sausages, and patties. The cutting room is divided into pork and beef. The pork goes to the left, the beef to the right, comprende?" Abdul pulled a white smock, a hair cap, two wooden dowels with meat hooks, and a pair of foam earplugs from a stack at the locker room entrance and handed them over to Pepper. Pepper pulled the smock over his work shirt and slipped on the hair cap.

"You're on a thirty-day probation," said Abdul. "After that, you're in. The Amalgamated Meat Packers Union fees are deducted from your check regardless of whether you go to the meetings or not, so it's worth it to go. You'll start in the unloading dock." Abdul nodded toward the factory floor. "Remember, my friend, beef to the right, pork to the left. The trucks arrive at five-thirty. Williams will get you situated."

Pepper put his lunch into locker two-one-two, made a quick mental note to avoid forgetting the locker number, and then headed to the loading docks. The workers slammed slabs of meat onto the metal tables and pushed them through the blades. A high-pitched buzz ripped through Pepper's ears. He noticed the other men wearing the foam earplugs and put his in at once, making the buzzing bearable. A horn blasted, and the men cleaned the machines and headed toward the locker room.

He saw Juan Carlo and Ronaldo walk through the door. Pepper nodded to the locker room, and the two men followed his gaze. The tired men shuffled out as the third shift ended, and then a new, invigorated group came in through the double-wide doors.

Jaun Calo and Renaldo exited the locker room wearing the white smock and carrying metal hooks. The three men waited for Williams. Then a horn blared, and the workers went directly to their stations. Pepper and the other two new hires stood out, and for a moment, that fear came over Pepper, starting in his gut and then inching its way up to his spine. If the foreman saw Pepper standing around, the foreman would think Pepper was a lazy Mexican. Pepper couldn't have that. So he sprung and searched the locker room for Williams. There is no Williams in the locker room, nothing there but a shower full of naked men washing the blood, bone, and meat chunks from their hair, nail beds, and ass.

He decided to go to the front desk. Maybe Mary had arrived and would help him. He opened the front doors, slid between the slits of the plastic curtain, and found Williams leaning over Mary's desk. Williams must've been telling a joke because Mary laughed as Pepper walked in. She smiled at Pepper, then batted her eyes at Williams.

"Alright, I get it. Time to clock in," Williams said with a smile. He rapped his knuckles two times on Mary's desk. "Come on, new hire, if Abdul sees you standing around, he'll chew my ass out for not putting you to work."

In the factory, Williams, Pepper, and the two brothers stood on the lip of the loading dock where trucks were backing up. The smell of the hot grease from the truck engines folded into the scent of the raw meat of quartered pigs and cows.

"Cantero, you and Juan-Calo work the beef, and Renaldo and I will work the pork," Williams shouted over the saws. "Now, pace yourself, boys. We got twenty trucks to unload today, and I don't need you passing out. Not on the first day." Williams paused. "Comprende?" Then he turned to pull open the loading dock gates.

The four men nodded.

"Que dijo?" Renaldo asked.

"You are gonna work the trucks with the pork, con El Negro." Pepper nodded.

Williams spun around and pulled the earplugs from his ears. "What did you say, Mijo?" Williams's voice cut through the factory noise.

"I said him with you," Pepper said while stressing his Mexican accent in hopes Williams would calm down from being called El Negro.

A horn rang through the air, and the gates of the loading docks opened. The truck drivers parked their trucks and shuffled out of the driver's seat and around back to open the trailer doors. Inside the trailers were stacks of quartered cows hanging from the large meat hooks attached to the trailer's ceiling. Juan Calo struggled and slammed his hooks into the cow's carcass. His right hook struck the cow's rib and bounced to the floor. He looked at Pepper, and Pepper signaled Juan Calo to watch him. Pepper slammed one hook into the rump and the other underneath the rib cage. He lifted with his stringy, muscular legs and pulled the carcass off the hook.

"Keep your wrist strong and pull it up, then towards you" Pepper demonstrated.

The carcass towered over the five-foot-five-inch Pepper. At first, he struggled to get the meat onto his shoulder but pushed up with his bent legs and hoisted the carcass into the air until it tipped over the fulcrum of his shoulder. (Years from now, Pepper would develop a fat callous on his right shoulder from all the halved cows he had hauled as a young man.) The weight of the beef almost knocked him over, and he realized that if he didn't move fast enough, he'd topple over. He almost ran from the trailer to the loading cart. The other men moved sluggishly, each step an eternity. They were beefer, heavier men than Pepper and could take the load without strain. After unloading each slab, they would take breaks and walk back to the trailer at an almost sloth-like pace. Pepper's pace doubled the other men's. Pepper had no choice. If he did not move quickly on his feet, the weight of the carcasses would topple him over.

Williams said something Pepper, but in truth, Pepper could not hear a thing over the sound of the saws, the earplugs, and William's southern accent.

He kept this pace all morning, rushing up the ramp, hooking the meat, and running back down to deliver the meat. His legs and back had turned into balled-up muscle knots, and his shoulder had gone numb after unloading the first few trucks.

Pepper stretched his legs and back during his lunch break. He lay on the bench in the lunchroom, then lifted his legs and pumped them up and down. He learned this old trick from an Indio at the rancho they both worked at. After stretching, his lower back released, and the knots in his thighs dissolved one at a time. He was ready for another round of meat hauling. Juan Carlo and Rodolfo stood around Pepper, watching as if they were witnessing something miraculous. A boxer catching his second wind.

"Told you to take it easy," Williams laughed. "You ain't the first hotshot around here to work himself to death."

After lunch, Pepper kept the same pace, and at times he sped up because if he stopped moving, even for a second, the cow's muscle, fat, and bone would topple him over.

Work at Payton's left him exhausted. But not once did he ever complain. What is it about us Mexicans accepting hard work as second nature. We live for it. Nothing like falling asleep after a long day of hard manual labor.

"He was a hard-working man," Monse once told me. "Work was the only thing he did right. But he was a worthless drunk and a lousy lover."

By the time I had come to live with my Grandparents, my Grandfather had stopped drinking. In his sobriety, he possessed a certain calmness and ease. Never once yelling at me. Yet, according to Monse, Pepper was a monstrous drunkard with bastard children all over the city. He carried his meat all around town, she would say.

I could never reconcile the Pepper I knew with the Pepper that haunted the sentences in her stories.

YOUR MOTHER IS A PUTA

One morning, while waiting for the bus to Zapata Elementary School, my Grandmother said, "Your Mom was a puta."

The morning rain had left the desert with the sweet smell of wet earth. Cars splashed about, sending waves of greasy rainwater up the banks of the sidewalk curbs.

Monse's words fell heavy into the pit of my stomach. Monse had used the word, *puta*, all the time. Every time we walked past a woman with lipstick or skin-tight clothes, Monse mouthed the word puta under her breath. Then, she'd pull me closer like she was protecting me from a would-be attacker. Puta was my grandma's foul word for the women she hated most, especially women that would catch Pepper's eye. She called Jesus's wife a puta. It drove my uncle crazy. He'd spend his next breaths explaining that Margeret made him happy. Monse would laugh and call Jesus a pendejo.

Monse never talked about my mom, Mercy. But that morning, she said my mom was a puta. Her face was as shocked as mine like she had accidentally blurted the words. The bus pulled to the curb before she or I could say anything. Some of the rain splashed onto my fresh-pressed khakis. Monse helped me up the first steps of the bus, something she hadn't done since first grade. She reached up to hug me, but I walked to the first empty seat as fast as I could. I sat next to Sally Diaz, the little girl everybody picked on for having a massive overbite. Some of the kids on the bus made kissing noises. Then the worst thing that could happen, did. My grandmother climbed onto the bus. All the kids stared up at her at once.

"Sharlie, ven aca." She waved me forward. I didn't want to go, my legs were lead. If I got up, the whole bus would laugh at me. I ducked behind the seat in front of Sally, but Sally reached down and grabbed me by the collar, and lifted me up as best she could. I looked into Sally's ratty eyes. Oh, Sally, with her big buck teeth hanging over her upper lip and dry crusty hands. All the seventh-grade boys made fun of Sally. They called her smelly-snatch Sally. They'd throw spit wads into her long curly hair and draw pictures of her big rabbit teeth.

"He's right here," Sally said in her goofy-ass buck-tooth voice.

Monse charged, grabbed me by my face, and planted a big wet kiss on my cheek. "I love you," she said, and bam, just like that, the entire bus, even the bus driver, broke out laughing.

On the way to school, one of the kids said, "Is that your fat ass mom, Charlie." Then another kid kicked the back of my seat. I tried to ignore the other kids by drawing in my notebook. Then one of the kids yelled, "Charlie, why don't you kiss Sally like you kissed your fat mom."

Sally looked over at me, and I could see the sweat blooming on Sally's forehead. The whole bus broke out, "kiss her. Kiss her. Kiss her."

Sally's face turned red, and I could feel the heat coming off her. I wanted to turn around and smack Peter in the fathead for kicking the back of my seat and making fun of Sally. Monse's brothers would have beat this Cheeto-breath bully to a pulp. I stood up and rolled my hands into tight fists. I wanted to say something like *Peter, you ain't shit*, then sock him in the mouth. Then it would be April, not Sally, that would give me a kiss for being so brave. My hands trembled with adrenaline. Peter had this look on his face; he was scared. Before I could swing my fists, the bus pulled onto the road, and the motion knocked me back into my seat. Peter laughed and kicked my chair again.

We had Sloppy Joes with canned corn and instant mashed potatoes in the cafeteria. A few of the kids from the bus chuckled when I walked past them with my tray. After eating, I went outside and played basketball with some of the other fourth graders. My stomach felt heavy. During P.E., the coach made us run laps. He timed us to see who could run the fastest. I came in fifth place in the sprint among the boys. Sally came in first among the girls. Then the coach made the fastest boy race, the fastest girl. Peter versus Sally. The coach blew the whistle, and Peter looked at Sally and said, "Don't trip over your buck teeth, Bugs Bunny." The entire class laughed, including me.

After all that running, my stomach felt worse. It felt like a can of yeasty biscuits was about to burst in my gut. I needed to use the restroom, but the last time someone used a toilet in the locker, Peter and his boys took a trashcan and dumped it all over the kid in the stall. Now he goes by Toilet Trash Teddy. I couldn't have that. So I held it in.

During science class, we used microscopes to find the chloroform in leaves. Then it was off to English class, where we learned about sonnets. By this point, my guts were ready to burst. The teacher, Mrs. Blumgarden, had begun the second verse of Shakespeare's 29th sonnet when my stomach clenched like a fist. I raised my hand and asked if I could go to the bathroom. School would be out in ten minutes, but that sloppy Joe needed out.

"Wait till I'm done with the Sonnets." She looked at me for half a moment, then returned to reading.

"I alone beweep my outcast state, And trouble deaf heaven with my bootless cries, And look upon myself, and curse my fate."

I felt something shift inside of me. I jumped out of my seat.

"Sit down, Mr. Cantero."

I begged to go to the restroom. The sweat had glossed my face, and my stomach rumbled with such fury that I thought the entire class could hear it.

"Sit down, sir, or I will have to send you to the office."

"Send me to the office then."

"I will after I have finished reading these sonnets. Now sit!"

She started the sonnet over. I looked around the room, trying to find anything to help me. My eyes locked with bucktooth Sally, and she mouthed, *sit down, mama's boy.*

I needed to run out of there. My stomach cramped. Something wicked this way comes. I sat to relieve the pressure bubbling over and out of my guts. My butt hit the chair, and my sphincter released a hot mess squirt. The mess filled my underwear and ran down my leg. I was smothered in hot shit. I took a deep breath and tried to imagine my guts going in reverse, sucking back up.

The smell crept up from my seat and wafted over the class. One of the girls sitting next to me covered her nose and mouth. "Ew, someone farted!"

The entire class broke out in laughter. My face turned beet red, and my heart pounded against my ribcage. I needed to get out of the class. I wanted to run for the door. But everybody would know the mess I had made.

I looked over at Sally. She sniffed the air, making her look like a rat smelling her next meal.

"Sally farted!" I pointed at her, then covered my nose. The entire class laughed. "Ew, Sally Buck-cheeks, you're so gross."

I grabbed my backpack and slung it over my elbows to hang low and cover my butt. Then I ran out of the classroom. Mrs. Blumgarden yelled something at me, but the bell rang and drowned her out. I ran to the bathroom and ducked into one of the stalls. I peeled my pants off and slowly lowered my underwear over my legs and ankles. I gagged at the smell. I had like ten pounds of shit in my underwear. I wanted to cry but sucked it up and stuffed my underwear into the toilet. I cleaned myself the best I could. I must've used half the roll trying to get the shit off of me.

When I flushed the toilet, the underwear and toilet paper got stuck. I could hear the kids walking down the hallway. So I flushed again. There could be no evidence of what I had done. The toilet water began to rise.

I flushed and flushed and flushed. The water rose up over the lip of the toilet and onto the tile floor. I pulled on my pants to get them up, but they had already soaked up the toilet water. The water poured faster and faster from the toilet. I jumped out of the stall with my pants still around my ankles.

Peter walked in and saw me with my pants around my ankles. He laughed.

"Damn, Charlie, put that little ding-a-ling away."

I pulled my pants up and charged past him. I didn't want to hear him laugh when he saw the mess I had made. I ran out of the restroom and down the hall. I was going to run all the way home, back to my Grandma Monse. But before I could clear the hallway, Mrs.

Blumegarden grabbed me by the arm and snatched me. She looked me in the eyes. Her eyes were furious and ready to erupt.

"You don't leave my classroom without being dismissed." She shook me hard, and my pants slipped around my butt cheeks. She looked down at my genitals and then looked away.

"Oh, Charlie, please pull your pants up." She dug her nails into my arm and jerked me back and forth like she was shaking the dirt from an old rug.

Mrs. Blumgarden walked me all the way to my bus and marched me on board. She pointed her middle finger at me and told me she would have to suspend me next time.

I sank into the green pleather bus seat. I watched as each of the kids got on the bus. Joey, Nancy, Vanessa, Jason, and Sally. When Sally saw me curled up in the chair, she turned her head up and away from me. Then I heard it. The high-pitched snarky giggle of Peter and his friends. My stomach twisted into knots as the laughter got louder and louder. The bus driver yelled at everybody to sit down.

The bus doors closed, and the bus crept out of the parking lot and into the street. I heard Peter laughing louder, then he called out my name. "Anybody see Charlie?"

I peeked out from behind my backpack. Across the aisle sat Sally Garcia looking right at me. I mouthed the words, *No, please.*

"He's back here, Peter." She waved Peter over.

I hid behind my backpack. Sweat came pouring down my face. My soiled underwear were hanging on a ruler. Peter poked his head out from behind the chair.

"Hey, Shit-pants, you forgot this." Peter waived the ruler and shitty wet underwear over me. The shit water dripped over my bag and splashed onto my shirt. My underwear on a stick looked like a surrender flag. I wanted to smack Peter in the face. But before I could swing, Peter flung the shitty underwear at me. Whop! The underwear landed smack on my chest. Shitty water splashed all over my face and on the chair. Everybody laughs. The entire bus shook from all the hooting and hollering. The bus driver slammed on the brakes. Turned around and yelled at us to be quiet. The kids settled down but continued to snicker and laugh. Even Sally Garcia laughed at me. The laughter would die down, then someone would make a fart sound, and everybody would roar.

I threw the wet shitty underwear under the seat. Let that bitch driver clean it up. As the students exited the bus, they would comment, "Later stinky" or "have a good afternoon, shit boy."

Sally Garcia called me an ass face, then laughed a big bucktooth grin.

When I got home from school, I tried to go straight into the restroom to wash up, but Monse stopped me and asked for a hug and a kiss. I had my backpack over my chest to hide any stains. I hugged her and split for the restroom. I cleaned myself off and changed into gym shorts and a T-shirt. I didn't want to jump into the shower because Monse would barge in and ask me why I had turned the shower on.

She had a stack of fried salty corn-dough gorditas and chocolate milk waiting for me. She waved me over to the table, and I followed instructions like a dog.

I took a sip from the warm chocolate milk. Monse would keep me safe. She would shelter me from the laughs and the finger-pointing.

"I'm sorry for what I said this morning."

She smiled down at me with a large toothy grin. I nodded my head. I had forgotten that she had called my mother a puta. My stomach tightened again.

"Mira Charlie, when you were a baby, your mother brought you to us." Monse ran her fingers through my hair. "You see, she needed help taking care of you. She was young, still a little girl, and needed help." Monse walked over to the kitchen and came back with a bowl. "That's how you came to live with us." She placed her meaty palm on my cheek and held my face up. She paused for a moment, then smelled her hand.

"Sharlie, did you roll around in shit today?"

She smelled her hand again, then whipped her head back. Her face balled up.

"I had an accident." The dining room blurred as

my eyes teared up. "The teacher wouldn't let me go to the restroom." I'm full-out balling now. "Then the kids found my underwear..."

Monse wiped her hand on her apron and then caressed my cheek.

"I'm the only one that loves you, Sharlie. I'm the only one that will protect you."

I sniffled, "What about Pepper and Jesus?"

"They don't love you like I love you."

She walked out of the kitchen and into the bathroom to set a bath for me.

When I finished eating my food, I went into the bathroom. The mirrors had fogged up, and I could smell the sweet smell of Mr. Bubbles in the bathwater. Monse sat on the toilet seat and spread the bubbles with her hand. She asked me to take off my clothes and to get in. I had a couple of He-Man action figures on the lip of the tub. Monse dropped them into the bathwater. I took my t-shirt off, followed by my shorts, then tip-toed to Monse. I looked down at the clouds of bubbles and saw my toys sinking to the bottom. The bathwater burned my foot as I dipped my toe into the tub. Monse pushed me on the small of my back. I grabbed my toys and started playing with them. He-Man versus Skeletor and Beast-Man. Monse lathered and rinsed my hair before leaving to make Pepper his dinner. Slowly the bubbles began to pop, and after thirty minutes, there were only a couple of islands of bubbles. He-Man had overcome Skeletor, and all felt right in the world.

"Make sure you wash your butt and your huevitos, Sharlie," Monse yelled from the kitchen.

I lathered up the washcloth and scrubbed my body. When I got down to my huevitos, I felt a tingle in my weenie. I had never felt this tingle before, but it felt good. It gave my stomach a tickle. I worked the cloth around my testicles and up the shaft, which had grown. I didn't know what was happening, but it felt secret and shameful. Sex education wouldn't be taught for another two years.

The tickle in my stomach climbed up to my chest. I continued to clean myself. The muscles in my legs tensed, and my toes curled. I needed to erupt, to shout out, to explode. Excitement rushed through my body, starting at my finger tips and toes and racing toward my erection. I released into the bath water, my stomach contracted, and my big toe twitched. I heard a loud gasp, and when I looked up, I saw Monse standing over me.

She had never hit me. Not even when I spilled her hair dye all over the living room carpet. But that afternoon, she slapped me across my wet face and called me a cochino before storming out of the bathroom. I grabbed my cheek, which pulsed with the sting of her beefy hand. Specs of white glob floated in the water and mixed with the remaining bubbles. I cried for a minute before unplugging the drain at the bottom of the tub.

Monse had brought a towel in, but she had dropped the towel on the floor before slapping me. I picked up the towel and dried off. Some of those globs of white had stuck to my legs. I tried to wipe them off with the towel, but they only smeared across my thigh. I patted my head dry and worked my way down my body. After drying my private parts, I noticed a small circle of red blood in the center of the towel. Maybe Monse had cut me when she slapped me, but I saw no blood when I inspected myself in the mirror. I looked down and saw the bloody tip of my penis. My heart dropped. I covered myself with the towel. On TV, they always say to put pressure on a bleeding wound. So I grabbed myself and squeezed. I prayed and begged God to make me whole. I swore I would never touch myself from that day on. I pulled the towel off my privates. The blood had clotted, and peeling off the towel caused pain to shoot up my body which sparked that tingle of pleasure I had felt while washing myself. I patted myself dry and thanked God.

I wanted to go straight to my room, but Monse stood in the hallway. She took one look at me and shook her head no. Then she called me a puñeton. I unfurled the towel so she could see the bloody rings in the center.

"Dios te castigo." She pointed up to the ceiling and wagged her finger. "He's always watching you. He knows."

I ran past her and into my room. I closed the door, then buried my face into a pillow. I cried and screamed into the pillow, trying to muffle the world.

An hour later, Pepper came home. I could hear

Monse talking to Pepper in the kitchen. My name came up several times, though I could not clearly explain what she told him. Pepper knocked on my door before entering. I had stopped crying and was playing with my toys. He walked over to the bed and asked me to sit beside him. I could not look him in the eyes. I wanted to cry again, but Pepper had taught me never to cry in front of another man. I took a deep breath and sat next to him.

"Sharlie," he said as he touched my shoulder. "When a boy starts to become a man, his body changes." His voice was calm and even-paced.

He held out his right pointer finger and wrapped his left hand around his fingertip.

"When a man pulls back on his weenie for the first time," Pepper cleared his throat and paused. "The skin attached to the tip of your weenie tears off, and sometimes the tip will bleed."

I closed my eyes and imagined the skin slowly tearing off the tip of my penis like Velcro pulling apart. I could hear the tearing sound, which echoed in my head.

"It's a normal thing, Sharlie. Nothing to feel bad about. Nothing to be ashamed about. If you want, I'll give it a look to see if everything is okay." He hugged me, and I felt the tears swell up again.

I stood up in front of him and lowered my shorts. He tilted his head and looked down at my privates. He nodded his head and gave a bit of a chuckle.

"You'll be all right."

As I pulled my underwear and shorts up, Pepper said that Monse had also told him what she said about my Mom."

I looked up at him, but he looked away.

"Mira, your Mom never had a father to raise her, to help guide her."

As I pulled my underwear and shorts over my privates, the elastic band of my underwear snagged against my privates. I had a moment of faint pain, but it was amplified by the idea of the sound of the Velcro skin ripping off the tip of my penis.

As Pepper sat there explaining why my mother wasn't a part of my life, all I could think of was that tender skin ripping off and dangling in my shorts.

Julieta

"Why do you drink so much?" Monse asks me as soon as I walk into her house. I hadn't seen her in a while, but Jesus called and told me I needed to check-in.

"I don't drink that much," I say. "Besides, why don't you judge your son instead of me? He's the asshole."

"And you're nothing like him? Because your mother left you on my front porch like a fucking dog."

I can see the red veins burn into the creamy white of her eyes. Her left pupil shines metallic with cataracts.

"Don't forget," she says. "You're the bastard grandson of Pepper. That's the only reason I took you in."

Sweat pushes through my pores, and I can hear my heart pump. I need to leave.

"The only re-re-reason that I came," I stutter, "was to let you know that Jesus stole the money from Pepper's funeral. He used it for his fucking truck or vacations. Or he spent it on his puta wife."

"He didn't steal it, *estúpid*," she says. "I gave it to him. Besides, it was only a couple hundred dollars."

"That's bullshit," and you know it.

"Larga te, you ungrateful bastard!" she shouts before moving in on me and slapping my face with the back of her hand. The clasp of her gold bracelet snags my cheek and cuts into my lip. The scratch doesn't bleed, but it burns like a motherfucker. I grab my mouth with both hands and run out the door. My lungs are on fire, and my heart pounds.

"Run, pinche chavala," she shouts from the front door. Then she gives me the sign of the cross and kisses her hand before throwing me a finger.

I jump into my '87 Ford Ranger, push the clutch in, and turn the key. The engine shakes, but the Ranger won't start. I pump the gas and try again. Nothing. Monse's staring back at me. Her smile is wide and toothless. I pop the parking brake, get out and push the truck down the driveway. The truck picks up speed, and I jump in and then pop the clutch. The engine skips and bucks and turns over. My truck's rear tires jump the curb across the street from Monse's house, and I know I've smashed into Mrs. Robles's garden. I speed off. Nowhere to go but to a bar.

The bar's not too far from my apartment. If I get tore-up, I can walk back. It's early for a bar, and the happy hour crowd hasn't shown up. I order a beer and sit at the counter. The Place is empty except for the bartender. He's leaning against the counter, reading a magazine, and drinking espresso. He didn't pay me much mind, and I didn't pay him much either. Instead, I focus on my own problems. Monse and Jesus. Pepper's lost money. I need a way out of this mess. No girl, no money, no family.

I hear Julie's voice from behind, and I might be tripping.

"Hi, babe."

My heart sinks down into my guts and sloshes around in the bile. It's a mirage, a hallucination, wishful thinking. No way Julie is here. The bartender, this slender long-haired guy, looks up. He's all smiles. He puts down his magazine and walks around the bar to hug her.

I don't want to look because I know what's next. My heart can't handle it. Julie is wearing her black dress, jean jacket, and Doc Martens that I gave her last Christmas. We had spent hours decorating her jean jacket, sewing on patches, and clamping in studs. She dyed her hair red, which makes her skin glow. She wraps her arms around this skinny jerk, and he lifts her off her feet. *Fuck you, guy. Fuck you.*

I want to run, but my beer is half full. I chug it. It's a dark beer and doesn't go down easy.

"You want your usual, Babe?" The bartender says.

He walks back around the bar and works on making Julie a smokey Old Fashioned.

"How you doing, buddy."

I nod and tuck my head down. I don't want Julie to notice me. I am invisible. *Please, God, let me disappear.* She sits a few barstools away from me, and I turn in the opposite direction, hoping she doesn't spot me. I do not want to see the car wreck that's about to happen to my heart. But I'm a glutton for pain. Welcome to the freak show.

"Charlie?"

Her voice is sweet and soft. I turn back and look up at her. I have my puppy dog eyes ready.

She gives me a big hug, and I try to stand up and lift her off her feet just like that dick bartender, but my movements are awkward and stiff. She pulls away and pats me on the back.

She introduces me as one of her old friends from High School. The bartender, Gustavo, smiles and looks over. He shakes my hand, his hand is soft like a girl's, but his shake is firm.

"How have you been? What's new?" Julie asks.

Her questions are coming at me too fast. I'm a raw nerve of emotion and heartache.

"I'm good," is all I can muster.

That's all I can respond with. Gus slides over her smokey old fashioned. She thanks him without even looking at him. Her eyes are fixed on me, and I am embarrassed. I am a slob.

"Come on, let's go sit over there,"

She points to a couch in the corner of the bar. I nod. She turns to Gus and tells him to bring us another round. Gus is all smiles. He's cool with me sitting next to his girl. Do I look that bad? Am I no threat to Gus and Julie?

I finish my beer and follow Julie to the couch. I

want to hold her hand. I want her to lead me to the couch like she's done thousands of times before, but I dare not reach for her hand, not in front of Gus. She gives me a big smile and looks at me before I sit. She wants to know how I'm holding up. She heard I had left the call center. I asked her about her job. She's working as an office manager for a tattoo shop. That's how she met Gus. He went in to get a Virgin Mary tattooed on his chest. She always loved tattoos. I never wanted to get any. She had a little red heart just above her right hip. We ordered two more drinks. When Gus brought them over, he kissed her on the mouth. I almost went full rage on the guy.

The happy hour crowd trickles in. Julie and I played this game that we used to play when we were together. We would make up stories about the people at the bar. For example, this couple walks in, and the woman is wearing a navy blue medical uniform. The uniform fits her tight, and you can see the curves of her body. The man that walks in holding her hand is dressed in dress pants that stretch over his bulge. He has a tie on, but it's loose, and the top button of his dress shirt is unbuttoned. They are both in their forties. They both have wedding rings. As they order drinks from the bar, the guy runs his hand along the woman's lower back, eventually working his way down to her butt. He rubs it a few times, then pats it with a soft spank.

Julie starts. That's not his wife. She's the new office liaison, and he's the young dentist that just joined the practice. They are both married and are unsure if this is just a fling or something more serious. They love their spouses, but the sexual energy between them is palpable. They like this bar because neither of their spouses would ever go to some little hipster bar in downtown El Paso. This bar reminds them of their college days. Tomorrow they'll decide to keep the relationship going. For tonight, they told their spouses that they had to stay for audits at work.

Not bad, I tell Julie. Married people are never that affectionate.

The night passes in a flash, Gus is too busy working the bar to pay us attention, and Julie and I are having a blast. She's inched closer to me, and I want to hold her hand. I want to kiss her. I can tell she wants to do the same. I want to ask her for her new number. Then that asshole Gus comes up to us right in the middle of having a good time. His shift is over. He sits down next to Julie, and she's caught in the middle. He asks her where she wants to eat. Then kisses her behind the ear. What a douche. He asks me if I want to go and eat with them and proclaims that any friend of Julie's is a friend of his. Again, what a douche. I'm too broke to go. Otherwise, I might've gone just to be with Julie a little longer. But I saw the horror in her eyes when he asked if I wanted to go too. As they walked out of the bar, he patted her on the ass, just like the couple from earlier.

Gus, the dick, left me holding the tab. And now I'm beyond broke. Payday is not for another week.

Mary

Growing up, my grandmother's words about my mom constantly scratched at the back of my skull. It wasn't so much that Monse had called my mom a puta. That was just the beginning. After that first day, Monse got meaner with her language. She'd compare trashy-looking women with my mother. Then she'd mouth some obscenity like puta or basura. I wondered how my grandfather handled having a child out of wedlock. I imagine it went something like this:

Before the sun had risen, Pepper slipped his white-boxer shorts over his thin waist and flat ass. He pulled a white t-shirt over his back, picked up his boots with one hand, and slid his polyester Wranglers over his bony legs. The early morning cast a blue shadow into Mary's apartment; everything looked alive and sharp.

"Wait," Mary whispered.

He pulled the first lock of the door. Its metal joint popped.

"No puedo," Pepper said, raising his finger to his lip to hush her.

"Please," Marry said. She wiped the crust from her eyes, smearing her already muddled makeup. "I need you with me today."

"You know I can't."

She stretched her arms, and her left breast fell out of the sheets, and Pepper froze for a moment. She threw the sheets off her body. He undid his belt buckle, mistaking her action.

"Can't you see?" she said, rubbing her hand on the bottom of her pot belly. Her body had changed, her breasts were full, and her belly hung just slightly over her waistline, accentuating the curve of her hips.

Pepper picked up his boots, then pulled the third lock to open the door. One of his boots fell out of his hands. He was already in motion, ready to jump into his canary yellow Maverick and drive off into the morning sunrise. Back to his wife and kid, back to his home. He felt like a stranger on a vacation that had lasted too long. He had missed his wife.

The sun rose over the mountains to the east and momentarily blinded Pepper. He shielded his face with his forearm, like Nosferatu, then ran down the apartment stairs. He jumped into his Maverick. The engine grunted and pulled, but it did not turn. He pumped the gas pedal three times and cranked it again. The engine whined like a piglet, then died. He put his car into neutral, got out of his car, and pushed the car backward. He could hear Mary yelling from the apartment door. He looked back and saw how the fresh sun made her glow. He had never seen her look so wild, so alive. Her eyes were embers of anger. She shook his boot at him.

She yelled down at Pepper. Her words were unintelligible, but you could hear the fury burning in her throat. She hurled Pepper's cowboy boot down at him. The boot's leather glistened in the light of dawn before the heel crashed through Pepper's windshield, spider-webbing the glass into a thousand tiny cracks.

Pepper jumped into his rolling car and slammed the clutch into reverse. Vah-room, the engine turned. He shifted into first, grinding his gears till the sound of crashing metal drowned out Mary's yells. His big toe had split open like a ripe tomato during his escape. It bled over the gas pedal, gluing his toe to the cold metal.

He had fooled himself long enough. Told himself that perhaps Mary had gained a little weight. Her young body had reached its limit. Now she had a beer belly because they drank almost every day. Maybe she plumped because of all the restaurant food they ate. She was always tired because she worked long hours. But deep down, he knew. He'd seen a woman's body swell into pregnancy. He knew the signs, and on the drive home, he mulled over the thought of having another son. He stared out of his windshield and into the fractured and cracked world of the southwest desert city. Life with the morning menagerie of people headed to work and school.

He took a deep breath, trying to suck in as much air as possible before facing his wife. He parked his car and sat momentarily, deciding whether to limp through the front door or fall asleep in his car. He hadn't been home for a couple of days.

He slithered into the front door, trying not to make a sound, trying to sneak past her and climb into bed.

Eggs, chorizo, and flour sat on the kitchen counter. A water kettle boiled on the stove, and a filter filled with ground coffee hung over a clay pot. He heard the swoosh of a flushing toilet. He ducked into his son's room and closed the door.

Pepper heard her walking down the hallway and cracked the door just enough to see her walk past. He noted how much weight she had gained, and for a brief moment, he thought about Mary.

Monse poured the boiling water over the strainer and into the clay jug. She turned on the comal to heat up the tortillas.

She made flour tortillas by mixing two parts flour, one part water, two tablespoons of Snow Cap lard, one teaspoon of baking powder, and salt. She kneads the dough until it comes together, usually about seven minutes. The dough becomes a large ball from which she pinches off smaller balls. The smaller ball gets rolled out with a rolling pin. Make sure to flour the countertop and rolling pin, or the dough will stick. Heat on a comal, and voila, fresh homemade tortillas.

She put the first tortilla on the comal, flipped it when it puffed with steam, pulled it off, and rolled out another tortilla. She had heard Pepper's car pull into the driveway and expected to find him drunk and passed out in the driver's seat as he had done many times before.

Monse had a different outlook that morning. Even though Pepper hadn't been home all night, he always came back to her. She took some solace in that idea. It gave her a ledge of hope to hang on to. She wore a dress made from a sunflower-patterned fabric that she loved so much. She also used the fabric to make curtains and a tablecloth. The dress was ill-fitting, and she wore it with pride. It took her four hours to make and sew the pattern together.

Though she knew Pepper had been out fucking around, she was relieved he had made it home. She would nurse his hangover. It felt good to be needed.

Pepper prided himself on being a truthful, honest man. But as he thought about Mary, a series of excuses, scenarios, and lies formed in his head. How could he handle two families?

Pepper himself had grown up without a dad. Pepper's father, Torongo, had several families, and Torongo visited Pepper and his mother on two occasions. Both times he asked Pepper's mother for money. He couldn't remember his father's face, just the silhouette of his father standing in the doorway. "Mijo, you are the man of the house now. Take care of your mom."

Pepper closed the door and looked down at his sleeping son, Jesus. Jesus was curled up in a blanket, thumb in his mouth, rosy cherub cheeks, and a slight smile. Pepper climbed the bed and put his arm around Jesus. Maybe he could pretend he had gotten home late and slept in his son's room. The doorknob jiggled, and Pepper closed his eyes, faking sleep. Monse walked in with a rolling pin in hand. She said something like "Mendigo cabron" or "Pinche cobarde." Then she hit his arm with the rolling pin.

"Vieja!" Pepper yelped, "It's me. Tu Amor."

She slapped him across the face. The flour on her hand clouded around Pepper, and a white handprint marked his cheek.

The smack woke Jesus, and he screamed a sharp squeal.

Before Monse could say anything, Pepper jumped to his feet, grabbed her by the neck, and slammed her head into the closet doors. The door caved in. "Vieja cabrona!" he yelled before punching her in the stomach. She knelt over from the blow. Jesus jumped out of his bed and ran at his father, swinging hard at his father's backside. Pepper spun around and slapped Jesus in the neck.

"Leave him alone!" Monse yelled.

Pepper pulled his leather belt from his waist and cracked it onto Jesus's back like a whip. Monse scrambled on the floor until she found the rolling pin. She got to her feet and lifted the rolling pin into the air. Pepper spun around and saw her. He stepped back and kicked her in the stomach. She fell to her knees again. Pepper whipped the leather belt across her back. One, two, three lashes. The belt cracked leather against leather. Jesus curled up in the corner of his room and cried out for his mother. Monse cried under the lashing, weeping and begging Pepper to stop. Pepper had gone rabid, his mouth foaming with curse words.

Her eyes had teared, and the world blurred. In that blur, she saw Pepper's busted and bloody toe. A beacon calling to her. She lifted the rolling pin and slammed it on Pepper's foot. His busted toe squirted puss and blood. Pepper swallowed hard. His eyes teared up. His eyeballs rolled into the back of his skull. The pain shot up Pepper's leg. He hopped out of the room, down the hallway, and into his bedroom, leaving a trail of blood and tears in the hallway.

The faucet's cool water relieved some pain until he poured hydrogen peroxide, and a bolt of hot electricity ran up his spine when he poured peroxide over the bloody pulp. When his toe stopped bleeding, he wrapped tissue around it. The tissue soaked up the blood.

He wobbled over to his bed and tucked into the sheets, careful not to hurt his toe. He fell asleep to the cries and whimpers coming from Jesus's room.

Pepper slept for six hours and awoke to the smell of sesame seed hamburger bread frying in a pan. His toe still hurt, and the blood had turned rust-brown. His unwrapped toe looked like a greasy smashed sausage link.

After wobbling into the kitchen, Pepper sat at the table and didn't speak. Monse formed a thick hamburger patty from the ball of seasoned ground beef. She used her rolling pin to roll out the meat, then tossed it into a frying pan. When the burger was ready, she put the plate before Pepper and went straight to her room.

He ate quietly, listening for Monse. He thought he heard her praying. As he chewed the burger, something jammed between his back molars. A pain surged from the nerves in his mouth and spread across his body. He jumped up from his chair, ran to the bathroom, and opened the medicine cabinet looking for floss but found none. His clumsy thick fingers prodded around his molar, rubbing his finger along his gumline until he came upon what felt like a sharp piece of bone. He pulled it out and felt instant relief in his mouth. He held the shrapnel in his palm, a little wedge of aluminum. His stomach cramped. A warning from Monse.

Pepper jumped on the toilet and stayed there for an hour. It felt like his guts had exploded. He shit out everything in a steady stream.

After his stomach settled, Pepper went to Monse's room, tapped on the door, and slowly opened it. The right side of her face was swollen, her hair doing a poor job covering most of the bruise. He tried to hug her, but she pulled away.

Is this what you brought me to El Paso for?" she rolled her hands into a fist.

"Mary's pregnant," Pepper said. He opened his hand and showed Monse the aluminum shrapnel.

Monse's eyes welled up with tears. She bit down on her lip so hard it bled, but the pain relieved her tears. She spits a bloody luggie into Pepper's face. He wiped the spittle and blood from his face and left her room. He limped into the kitchen, opened a beer, and sat at the table drinking while listening to Monse sob.

PACK OF WEENIES

The spring of '61 was unusually fresh and cool, unlike the year before when the heat had hit so hard Pepper felt like he was going to boil over. That spring, the spring of 61', the Cantero's felt, for a brief moment, that they might be happy. They had escaped the crushing horror of poverty and uncertainty that had held on to them so tight in the years after they had crossed that cursed line of the U.S.-Mexico border. And for that brief moment in '61, Pepper, Monse, and Jesus could all take a deep breath and relax..

Then a strange rumbling began at the Payton Meat Factory. The Amalgamated Meat Packers lost some pension money due to a restructuring of payment options. The union meetings got so heated that they often ended in a fistfight.

At first, Pepper was against the Amalgamated Meat Packers strike. He had no concept of pensions, nor had he ever had one before being hired at Payton. For Pepper, the idea of getting paid without working seemed unfair.

"Why should the company pay us, even after we've stopped working here?" he asked. "Yo voy a trabajar hasta que ya no pueda. Descanso cuando me muera."

Descanso cuando me muera had become Pepper's favorite mantra in the early days of living in America. His mantra kept him sharp, for he knew he could outwork any lazy gringo. He repeated his mantra when tired and sluggish.

Plenty of employers were willing to take a man like Pepper up on the offer of working till you're dead, and the Payton Meat factory was no different. They gave Pepper as much overtime as his small frame could handle. Sometimes Pepper would work twenty hours straight. He'd go home, shower, eat, take a four-hour nap, and be back at it in the morning.

Some of the more patient union members took the time to explain to Pepper how a pension worked. They explained that the money they were about to lose was, in fact, money that had been deducted from their check. His hard work and pay were being saved in a fund so that he could retire one day. He might have been dim by some standards, but he understood how thieves operated. The company he worked so hard for, the Payton Meat Factory, wanted to use him up, not unlike those dead cows they had strung up and quartered. So, after much thought, he sided with the Amalgamated Meat Packers and helped plan the strike. He put down his meat hooks and picked up a union picket sign.

The Summer of '61 had come with the vengeance of desert heat. The entire month of June had a record heatwave. Every day was over a hundred degrees, except one weekend in late June when it rained.

The Strike had knocked Monse and Pepper on their ass. Desperation came roaring back into their lives and snatched the breath from their chest. They thought the hard days were over. After the fifth week of the strike, they realized that desperation had laid dormant, waiting for the perfect moment to snap its jaws.

Pepper stood in line with his fellow A.M.P.U during the strike's first week. members under that hot desert sun. It felt more like a chain gang than a protest. Nothing romantic about the strike of '61. There were no women with flowers in their hair, no newspaper articles about the brave men, nothing but a bunch of half-starved Mexicans, a few white guys, and one black guy. They stood at the factory's doors from sun up to sun down. Some trucks pushed through, but not enough for Payton to turn a profit. The workers locked hands and stood their ground. They had been through worse.

Sometimes the meat would rot in the trucks. The unbearable stench stank up the neighborhood. All the warehouse district smelled like a rotting pig. The flies were thick as smoke, and they swarmed over the factory.

Some of the members brought burritos or sandwiches. But after a month, food had gone scarce, and the bellies of the A.M.P.U. Members rumbled with the fear that they had made a colossal mistake.

Then Payton brought in the heavies, strike-busters with fat necks and thick wrists. The strike-busters charged through the picket line and smashed any A.M.P.U member in the way. They fought for two weeks. Pepper and the other A.M.P.U members held their ground. Even though the strike-busters would get through. Then Williams joined the picket line, and production stopped for a week. Williams had boxed in his youth, and those strike-busters had no clue what hit them. Williams loved smashing his fists into the strike-busters. He took particular joy in beating the crap out of the strike-busters that called him nigger.

It got to the point that the cops had to come out and stop the brawls. Fighting the strike busters carried on for five days. The A.M.P.U had won most of the clashes, and pork product production had stopped. Nobody had gotten seriously hurt beyond a scrapped knee, bloody lip, black eye, broken wrist, and two concussions. Pepper developed a strategy for the violence. He would hang back and take in all the action, watching the AMPU members fight with the scabs. As soon as a scab was on the floor, Pepper would run over to kick them in the ribs or step on their hand.

Of course, Payton Management had to bring in some real bruisers, thick-skinned ex-cons, bar brawlers, and dirty boxers to break up the strike. One of the more ruthless strike-busters hit Juan Calo so hard that Juan Calo's eye bulged out from the socket. An ambulance had to be called in. The Herrold caught wind of the story. The headline read: Rowdy Factory Workers Prevent Food from Being Delivered.

On that fourth day of fighting, Pepper came home all bruised up. He had a swollen lip, two black eyes, and a large gash on the top of his head. He cried into Monse's lap. The job had defeated him. The union's demands had defeated him. And he questioned if they had gotten too greedy. He had finally found some stability, and now it was all gone. Hauled away in a truck full of pork. He damned Payton and the Meat Packers. If he had just stayed working the line and kept his head down, he would have a job and wouldn't be hurting from that ass-whooping he took. He promised never to return to the Payton Meat Company. The strike-busters had won.

The picket line dispersed, and most of the men found other jobs. Some worked construction, but most returned to the fields, picking cotton or chile. Pecan season had already come and gone.

The Cantero's fridge and cabinets were empty within a month, save for a few cups of rice, flour, eggs, and a sack of beans.

To survive, I imagine, Pepper worked all types of jobs. He landscaped the new houses going up on the east side, picked chile from Socorro's dusty fields, cleaned parking lots in Downtown El Paso, and built the frames for houses. The work came in unstable waves, weeks where things had dried up all over town, then a sudden crash of people needing their yards cleaned or a farm needing extra hands. The times were as tight and arid as the desert valley.

It got so bad that Pepper sold his beloved yellow Ford Maverick. Before turning over the keys, Pepepr drove the car to the top of Scenic Drive. He sat on the hood of his Maverick and starred out to the sea of lights. From Scenic Drive, you can look down the valley where the line between Mexico and the United States blurs into one large city. He thought about returning home. He thought about taking his wife and son back to Mexico. He could find work there busting broncos or slaughtering pigs. He also thought about his brother. It had been his brother, Palacio, that had wanted to move to the States. Palacio had wanted to start a ranch. Palacio wanted to drive chrome-trimmed cars. Pepper closed his eyes and remembered sitting at that lousy cantina, Chacha's, drinking beer and whiskey as Palacio explained the possibilities of the United States to Braulio.

"And the pinche güeras, carnal, son pero buenotas pa cochar."

America was his brother's dream. At that moment, Pepper realized he had left Aldama because he owed his brother. He had to stay in the U.S.A, a promise he made the day they buried Palacio. He had to endure until his debt to his brother was paid.

The sale of the car kept them above water. He had enough to pay the landlord, buy groceries and even buy Jesus a baseball. Then things got really lean, down to the bare bones lean. He sold the calfskin boots that his brother had given him. And with that, any semblance of pride left Braulio "Pepper" Cantero.

Monse had saved as much as she caught wind of a possible strike. She hid her cash in a mason jar, mostly loose change. She hid the jar behind the folded clothes in Jesus's dresser. Her saving had been a year-long effort. She saved money by short-changing Pepper after every grocery store visit. A dollar here, eighty-six cents there, but then he got savvy and started checking the receipts.

She knew the exact amount in that jar, two-hundred forty-six dollars and thirteen cents, one of the many secrets she kept from Pepper.

During the AMPU strike, my grandmother slowly picked away at the jar. She'd take five for groceries and two for Jesus's school uniform. Finally, she used the last thirteen dollars and seventy-two cents to pay the El Paso Electric Company.

They were so hard up for cash that her once buttery flour tortillas became watered-down crapes so thin the sunlight poked through them.

One day, standing in line at Mata's Grocery Store, she realized she didn't have enough money to pay for her groceries. She went over the amount of change she had in her purse. The butcher knocked his fat knuckle on the countertop and told her she had to pay or get out of line.

She turned back and saw the line of people that had formed behind her. One of the men in line, a squat mahogany-skinned man, had the same curly wool hair as her brother, El Gitano. She thought back to her days at the family ranch and remembered the thick iron smell of a pig her brothers and father had bled and gutted for roasting. The pig's intestines smelled like shit, and they made a loud smacking sound against the hard dirt floor when her brother had gutted the pig. She stood in horror until her father waved her over. She did not want to get close.

"You have to learn the rancho, Mija." He told her. "Now get over here and scoop up the guts, squeeze out the shit, and take them to your Mom so she can rinse them out for Menudo."

Her stomach cramped at the memory, which collapsed, returning her to the butcher's counter. The butcher tapped again, his face a knot of anger. For the first time in her life, Monse had gone hungry, a true hunger that builds over days. This type of hunger gives you a headache in the back of your head. It sucks your stomach up into the cavities of your ribs. This is the hunger you feel when all you've had to eat is half of a tortilla, which you portioned into two meals.

Monse looked up at the butcher. He had turned red with anger.

"I am going to have to skip you."

"Pinche gusano, don't you ever talk to me like that," sneered Monse. "I'll pay cuando me de la pinche ganas. And if you have a problem with that, I'll talk to your Manager, or better yet, I'll have my husband come down and talk to you."

The cashier's red fat face softened, and he apologized.

She turned back and said she would return some of the items because they were better priced at Holland's. Monse made sure she said it loud enough for everybody in line to hear.

She ordered a dozen red hot dogs. The butcher nodded and smiled at her before wrapping the weenies in butcher paper. "I'm gonna give you a discount," the butcher made the okay sign with his index finger and thumb. "I'm sorry they rushed you."

Monse snatched the bag of weenies from the butcher before walking away with her head held high. Then she walked by the produce, picked up an apple, smelled it, and shook her head as if to suggest that the fruit was of poor quality.

She walked around the store, taking her time with her shopping. She didn't have much, maybe a dollar-fifty at best, but she carried herself like she could afford to buy out the whole store. Then she hid in the far left corner of the store, looked around to make sure no one was watching her, slid the package of weenies under her shirt, and tucked them into the folds of her armpit. The cold franks sent a shiver down her spine. She bought a loaf of bread for forty-two cents. The cashier let her cut the line.

Monse headed to the bus stop across the street. The weenies kept her cool on the bus ride home, but they warmed to body temperature when she got home. That night, she chopped up four weenies and scrambled them with the last three eggs in the fridge. Jesus complained because there was no ketchup, but he wolfed down those eggs nonetheless.

I imagine she wept that night, the taste of hot-dog weenie still on her breath. My Grandmother's pride might have been her only refuge in a new country, where she neither spoke the language nor understood its workings. And now she had lost even that.

A Fith Of Whiskey and a Gun

Pepper nervously sipped his whiskey and chased the bitter-burning liquid down with a gulp of his beer. If Pepper wasn't at work, you could find him at Gorditas, a shitty dark and damp little bar wedged between the Payton Meat Factory and the Action West Jeans Factory. The inside of Gorditas was heavy with cigarette smoke. Kool and the Gang's *Summer Madness* spun on the jukebox, and on the long hot August night, it felt like the world had slowed down.

The bartender came back around and poured Pepper another whiskey. Pepper tapped on his beer, signaling for another one. The bartender returned with the beer and said, "some one's on the phone looking for you."

Pepper reached over the bar and took the receiver. Myra was on the other end of the phone. Pepper Answered. "You have a little girl!" Myra said. "Mary gave birth, and your daughter's beautiful."

Pepper flashed a big old toothy grin and shouted to the bar, "I have a little daughter, a little girl!" Pepper shouted. "A round para todos!"

And the bar cheered and patted him on the back. The other factory workers and some of the waitresses congratulated Pepper. Some even shook his hand as they walked to the bar for their free drink. A whiskey and coke. A Coors. A shot of Mezcal. By midnight, the world had turned into a smear of hot breaths and hollow congratulatory phrases.

At Gorditas, you could pay a waitress to hang out with you if you bought them a watered-down, overpriced drink. They'd sit with you and rub on you, whispering into your ear how sexy you made them feel. After about fifteen minutes, they'd finish the drink. You could keep the party going if you bought them another drink, which Pepper did all night till the bar closed. One of the waitresses walked him to his car. She stole his wallet. Of course, Pepper was too drunk to remember which waitress stole his wallet. But in the morning, none of that would matter. His first daughter had been born.

It's hard to tell how Pepper made it home that night. Maybe some instinct had kicked in from years of driving home from the factory and the little bar next to it. He prayed as he drove home. His car swerved through the back roads.

He shoved through the front door and went straight for the kitchen. He opened the refrigerator and grabbed the brown bag lunch his wife had made him for the following day's work. He tore through the two burritos, then crashed around for a moment. Under his drunken gaze, the floor slid back and forth, and the kitchen walls swayed while Pepper tried to balance himself on the counter.

The waitress back at Gorditas had him all hot and bothered. She had rubbed up on him just long enough to get him to spend all his money. He didn't mind. Tomorrow, after the hangover, he'll look into his wallet, then, half confused, he will ask, "How much did I spend?" The memory of the night will creep through like the desert sun peeking through a curtain. The haze of browning out.

Pepper bounced around the hallway until he entered my Grandmother's bedroom. He stood at the end of the bed, watching her sleep. His eyes blurred in and out of focus. Monse was asleep on her side, her heavy chest rising and falling to a gentle snore. He pulled his belt off and slid his pants and underwear down over his boots. The room smelled sweet, like anise.

His movements were clumsy and brutish while rolling Monse onto her back. She was a heavy sleeper and kept on snoring. He pulled her underwear to the side before crawling up on her. His breath heavy with whiskey. The smell shocked Monse awake. She pulled away, squirming under Pepper. He kissed her with his hot whiskey mouth. She tried to yank her head away, but he covered her mouth and nose with his right hand, his strong hand. He pinned her down to the bed. She bit, kicked, and scratched at him, but his nerves were gassed with booze. The pain only excited him more.

She tried to imagine anything better, some other place. Still, Pepper's hot breath kept pulling her back, yanking her from childhood to the very violent present. She thought of her Mother and her Brothers. She thought about working in the puesto, selling jamonsillo. Back to the present, Monse heard her mother whisper. *Mija.*

When he finished, he rolled off of her.

She kicked him hard in the back, and he crashed onto the floor, smacking his head on the corner of the oak nightstand. He groaned at the pain growing from the corner of his head. He sank deep into the carpet, too dizzy to stand, too tired to stay awake. He closed his eyes, and the world vanished into the dark of his dreams.

Monse wiped her tears and sat up at the edge of the bed. She looked down at his half-naked body, a mess of bony elbows, knees, and ribs. She wanted to stomp on him and crush his skull with her heel.

He started dry heaving. And for a moment, Monse saw an out, an escape from this beast. She could return home, back to Mexico. Her family would forgive her for leaving. All she had to do was hold a pillow over his mouth and let the night take him. Before she could finish her thought, he threw up all over himself. Monse jumped out of bed and stood over him. Watching him vomit. His body convulsed, jerking back and forth, heaving and shaking. Yak, yak. The red vomit covered his face and his nostrils. He gasped for air through the thick hot goo. Monse watched as Pepper's face turned purple like a bruise. In her heart, she wanted to return to Aldama with her son. A new life without Pepper. Her family would take her back. She missed her brothers and her father. If her father had known how Pepper had treated Monse, her father would have killed Pepper. All these ideas flashed through her mind, a cacophony of ideas and possibilities.

A small tear rolled down his cheek.

She thought about her son, remembering when Pepper taught him to loop a rope around a chair. "Eso, Mijo." Her son, Jesus, had wrangled the chair on his second try. All the while, Pepper made these horse animal noises. That one happy moment angered Monse so much that she kicked Pepper in the ass. He twitched but did not open his eyes. She put her foot underneath his lower back and rolled him onto his side. The vomit and bile poured out of his mouth onto the red carpet. Then he gasped for air. Breathing hard. But never did he open his eyes. Not once. She slapped him on the cheek, imprinting her hand on his face. He didn't wake. With his boney ass out in the cold air, his pants and underwear still around the cowboy boot of his right leg, she stomped on his thigh. She had never hated him more.

In the morning, Pepper woke up to find himself covered in piss. His head throbbed and thumped, and his body felt like a crushed can. The pungent vomit forced him to dry heave. His empty stomach tightened, and his body cramped tight. He called out for Monse. No answer. Then he called out for his son, Jesus. No answer. The world was a muddled mess, and in that cold puddle of piss, the previous night began to unveil itself. He recalled being at Gorditas and celebrating, though the reason for celebrating escaped him. He pulled himself from the primordial juices of his stomach. He inched his way up the bed and eventually onto his feet. He pulled his boot off and slipped off his soiled underwear. Each step sent an electric jolt through his skull. He hobbled over to the restroom, his right leg aching and bruised. He rinsed his mouth with the faucet water, then looked in the mirror and saw a blood-shot dried-out version of himself staring right back. The bruise from a hand was red on his cheek.

It wasn't until he was in the shower that he remembered his girlfriend had just given birth to their daughter, Mercy. He rolled her name around in his mouth. Mercy. He had never heard the word before, but he liked its sound when it left his heavy accented lips. Despite the world of pain, a smile crept across his face. He had a daughter, a little girl he would love and hold. Even the pain of his hangover could not compare to the joy he felt deep in his mind and heart. He felt Mercy all the way down into his soul.

After his shower, he cleaned up the vomit by throwing his wet towel over the mess. He shaved, dressed, combed his hair, took four aspirins, drank two beers, and his hangover had shrunk to a mild headache. Though Monse and Jesus had left the house, Pepper had no worry that they would stay gone. Monse always came back. After all, where would they go? Monse had no family or friends, at least not on this side of the border. She had no one but Braulio.

On his way to visit Mary, Pepper bought his little girl a bouquet of roses and a small white teddy bear. Before entering the hospital, Pepper took in a deep breath. His mouth tasted like whiskey and old leather shoes. He wanted to send Monse back to Mexico so he could start over with his new American wife. And together, they would raise their daughter. They would have more children, and he and Mary could grow old together. He entered the room with excitement in his eyes and a smile on his face. Mary had her left breast out, feeding their daughter, Mercy. When Mary looked up at the doorway and saw the shabby hungover Pepper standing there, she winced.

"What the hell do you want?" She covered herself up.

"I want to see my daughter." Pepper held out the roses and teddy bear.

Mary bowed her head and waved him foreword. He placed the flowers on the rolling tray next to Mary's bed. He reached out to grab his little girl, but Mary pulled her away.

"What does your wife think about this?"

Pepper shook his head no. "Can't we just be happy? Us three. In our own little world? Can't we just love?"

"Is that the same line you told your wife?" Mary furrowed her eyebrows.

Pepper sat at the edge of the bed. He shrugged his shoulders, and in the most serious voice he could muster, he explained to Mary that he would send Monse back to Mexico. Pepper would ensure they were cared for and send them money, but he wanted to be with Mary and his little girl. He promised to wed her, buy them a home, and be a good man. He could start over.

"What if I don't want you? What if I found someone else? Someone who could take care of us and never leave us." She took in a deep breath.

Pepper tried to muster up some tears. He blinked and rubbed his eyes, trying to show her he cared. He needed to show her that he loved her. But his body had dried out. When he reached over to kiss his daughter, Mary slapped him. "Don't you touch her, you fucking drunk!"

When Pepper pulled up, he saw bags of clothes slumped over on the front porch. As he walked past the bags, he kicked one of them before charging into the house. He found Monse cleaning the restroom.

"Aren't you leaving with your *puta*?" yelled Monse.

Pepper didn't say anything.

"I know your daughter was born yesterday," she hissed. "*Me lo dijiste anoche cuando me estab as chingando*."

She threw him a finger, motioning like she had rammed it up his ass. He felt something tickle his anus and push up into his guts. The sensation hurt him so much that he ran out of the house and tripped over the bags of clothes. He picked himself up, dusted off his cowboy shirt, and headed for his last place of refuge. Gorditas.

The bar's stale-air bit into his nostrils, and the smell of last night's sweat, cigarettes, and beer were slathered with the ammonia used to wipe down the counters, the floor, and the toilet.

During the day, Gordita's filled with geriatric patrons, men and women in their late seventies that took drinking seriously. Some dressed like cowboys. Others were so old they needed an oxygen tank. Gordita's served as the adult daycare for these old busted souls. By two o'clock, the gaggle of nurses would usher the viejitos out and take them home. And that's how they spent their twilight years, drinking at a languid pace, waiting for the day they could fade away into the sweet hereafter.

Pepper sat at the bar and ordered a beer and the greasiest cheeseburger on this side of the Rio Grande. He watched two of the older men shoot some pool. Each game took at least forty-five minutes. The old men would take breaks to sit and huff on oxygen tanks throughout the game. The nurses would pat their backs and give them a sip of beer.

The waitress handed Pepper his beer and then brought out his burger. She wasn't as attractive as the waitress from the night before. Still, nonetheless, compared to the fat old nurses and the pickled old men, this waitress was the best and only thing to look at in the bar. So Pepper gave her a big smile. The waitress walked from behind the bar to deliver two more beers to the viejitos at the billiards table. They thanked her by kissing her hand and tipping her a couple of dollars. Pepper eyed the waitress's thick ankles, the curve of her thighs, and the small of her back. She reminded him of a young Monse, not the tired, overweight woman that had thrown him out, but the mouthy young girl everybody called La Avispa.

The waitress rang up the two beers and put her

tips into a plastic pitcher beside the register. Her prize at the end of her shift.

Pepper lifted his burger, the grease and mayo dripping onto the counter. Before he could take a bite, a voice interrupted him.

"What you eating, young buck?"

A man wrinkled like a prune and dark as ebony sat at the barstool beside Pepper. Pepper hadn't noticed him when he first sat at the bar.

"They call me Juney," the old man said.

Juney reminded Pepper of his coworker, Williams. They both had the same long thick fingernails and tattered hands.

Pepper turned back to his burger and took a bite. He thought about how angry he felt when Mary told him she and Williams had dated.

"Are you telling me que ese pinche negro te cocho?" he shouted at Mary.

She had pulled a pillow across her body, hiding behind it as Pepper paced back and forth, throwing his arms in the air, stomping and cursing. Mary stood up. Pepper grabbed her by the arms and shook her violently.

"I never want to see you again, you piece of shit," Mary yelled. "You little verguilla motherfucker!"

He remembered the snap of his leather belt as he unbuckled it and whipped it from his pant loops.

“Stop,” she shouted.

He charged her, but a pounding at the door startled him out of his rage.

“You okay, Mary?” Shouted the neighbor’s voice from the other side of the door. “I called the police.”

Pepper re-looped his belt and hooked the buckle. He swung the front door open and found an old woman with a wispy gray mustache standing there looking at him with a dead eye that was once brown but had glazed over with a milky membrane. Her other eye was as fierce as a desert hawk.

“A tí que te importa?” he asked as he blew past her.

The woman raised her right hand, and a black rosary hung from her fist. “Hijo de la chingada,” she sneered.

Pepper took another bite of the burger and recalled his fight with Williams.

The morning after Mary told Pepper of her past relationship, Pepper arrived to work half an hour early. He was heaving madly, thinking a black man had slept with Mary. When Williams walked into work, he was all smiles. Pepper snarled and clenched his meat hooks. He wanted to swing the meat hooks at Williams, dig them into Williams’s back, and lift Williams off the ground like the pig carcasses hauled from the slaughterhouse trucks.

Instead, Pepper focused all his anger on unloading the first trucks. He dug his meat hooks into halved pigs and cows, lifted them off the truck's hooks, and ran them to the cutting tables.

"Slow down, Braulio," said one of the workers. "We can't keep up."

Pepper ignored him.

Pepper worked through all the breaks, including the lunch break.

After lunch, Williams went over to Pepper and asked him to slow down.

"You're making us all look bad," said Williams. "Including your buddies from Mexico."

Pepper did not say a word. He dug his hooks into the next carcass, lifted it onto his shoulder, sized Williams up, and ran down the ramp. He dumped the carcass at one of the cutting tables. Not even the guys working the saws could keep up with Pepper. The carcasses were piling up. Even the cut guys asked him to slow down, but Pepper wasn't having it. He would never slow down. He had grown tired of all the men and women that had held him back and asked him to go slow. Lesser men, like Williams. The only one Pepper responded to was Abdul, the foreman. When Abdul asked Pepper to slow down, Pepper promised he would but kept his pace anyways. Then Williams did something drastic. He stood in front of Pepper, keeping him from working.

"You're like a fucking hot pepper that won't stop burning my ass," said Williams. "Calm your shit down before I sit you down."

Abdul ran over to them. Angry and tense, Pepper held the two hooks down at his side, ready to pounce on Williams. Abdul jumped between the two men, "What the hell's going on here?"

"This negro huevon stands in my way," Pepper snarled. "He's not letting me unload the truck. He says I need to slow down."

"He's gonna hurt himself, Boss," Williams pointed to Peppers hooks.

"Clock out, both of you," said Abdul. "I don't want to see either of you for the rest of the week."

At home, Pepper asked Monse to draw him a bath. She could see it on his face; this world had defeated him, and he needed a break. Pepper was exhausted. Monse did not say a single word to him. Instead, she jumped up from playing cards with Jesus and went to the bathroom to draw him a warm bath. She lay his razor, shaving brush, mirror, and soap on the lip of the tub. The steam had fogged the room. She knew that Pepper liked to shave. Perhaps the razor's rasp or the soap's smell soothed him. She also placed some *yerba buena* leaves into the tub. The sweet aroma filled the room.

The hot water soothed his sore legs, shoulders, and back. The steam and smell of *yerba buena* opened his nasal passages. He soaked for a moment before Monse lathered a washcloth and rubbed the cloth on his back, neck, and chest, then she left the room.

He grabbed the shaving brush, studied its thick horse bristles, and swirled it over the soap bar. The horsehair cooled his hot face. He then dragged the razor across his stubble and shaved. After the bath, his muscles relaxed, and he was hungry for the first time since leaving Mary's.

Monse had already started on some food. The house filled with the beefy iron smell of liver and onions frying in a pan.

After drying off and dressing, he sat at the kitchen table with his shoulders slumped over.

"Me traes una cerveza?" he asked Jesus.

Jesus's chubby ass shook as he ran to the fridge.

Pepper wolfed down his liver and onions, slammed his beer, and left the house. He did not say a single word to Monse, not even a thank you.

He drove down El Paso Street to Dave's Pawnshop. The clerk was already lowering the front gate when Pepper pulled up. Pepper jumped out of the car and begged Dave to make one last sale.

Pepper had purchased several heavy caliber handguns and rifles from Dave, prompting Dave to show him a .38, then a .32.

"I want it to fit in my boot," said Pepper. "Something I can toss if I have to."

Dave pulled a Ruger Single-Six .22 caliber revolver from his safe.

"It's my gun," said Dave, "but I'll sell it."

Pepper held the gun in his hand; it felt lightweight and balanced in his meaty palm. He slid it down into his boot. Then paid Dave Eighty-two dollars and twelve cents.

The following day, Pepper rapped the gun in a brown paper bag and tucked it into the glove box of his Maverick. At work, Pepper paced himself, but even at a steady and slow pace, Pepper unloaded the trucks faster than the other workers.

"Them cows get the best of you?" said Williams during their first break. "You ain't moving at the same speed."

"Shut up, nigger," hissed Pepper.

"Is that right? You and I are gonna have some business to settle after work," said Williams. "I suggest you save your strength for the ass-whooping I'm going to give you."

After work, Pepper changed from his blood-stained smock into his Pearloid buttoned cowboy shirt. He walked to his car, pulled out the .22 from the glove box, and tucked it into the front of his pants. Pepper hid on the passenger side of William's orange Volkswagen van. When Pepper heard the keys go into the driver's side door, he jumped out from the side of the van.

"Aqui tengo para acabarte, puto," Pepper said.

"Cool it," shouted Williams when he saw the

gun. "I was only kidding about fighting after work."

It was unclear if that was true. It's hard to tell if a man's being honest when a gun is pointed at him.

"No more shit about how I work," Pepper said in a thick Mexican accent. "I can't stand with the cows on my back, so I have to go fast, or I'll fall."

"Keep it cool," Williams said. "To each his own, but we can't keep up. You have to understand that."

"No bullets," Pepper laughed.

Pepper opened the gun and exposed six empty chambers. He tried to spin the chamber like in the Westerns, but the damn thing didn't turn. "It's over between you and Mary, understand."

Williams shook his head, "it never really started."

Pepper flashed his big ol' smile.

Back at the bar, Pepper finished his delicious greasy burger. Juney smiled his toothless gums at the waitress and signaled for a beer.

"You want one too, young buck?" Juney asked.

The two sat at the bar, drinking all afternoon.

The thought of losing Mary did not enter Pepper's mind until he stumbled to his car, turned the ignition, and realized he had nowhere to go. He swerved around the city streets until he crossed the border into

Juarez. He felt something calling him, and he missed the town he grew up in. He missed his Mexico. And that's when the idea hatched in his inebriated brain to leave his wife in Aldama after her cousin's wedding. She could spend some time with family, and he would promise to return in a week. Maybe one day he would, but only for a short visit.

Monse Refuses to Cook on Thanksgiving.

Monse refuses to cook on Thanksgiving. Maybe she's depressed?

"I'm not going to cook anymore," she says, not without my Viejo here. No me importa el Thanksgiving de los pinche gringos."

"Ma, it's not about that," I say. "We just want to get together, you know? Family status."

"No."

"I'll help," I say. "I'll make the masa for the tamales."

"I don't care," she says.

I wrap my arms around her shoulders, resting my cheek on her curly silver hair. She shrugs me off.

"Sit down," I say. "I'll make the food for once."

"You," she laughs. "You don't know how to make anything, Estúpid."

"What are you talking about, Jefita?" I say. "I'm a cook."

"A cook?" she says, "more like a marijuano. And besides, being a dishwasher at a restaurant doesn't make you shit."

"Go sit down before I leave," I say.

She turns around, balls up her fists, and then shakes them at me.

"Don't you threaten me, cabrón," she says.

She jabs at my side, hitting me between the ribs, and the pain tickles and startles me. I grab her wrists and pull her arms up.

"Let me go," she says.

"Then stop hitting me."

She cries, and I let her wrists go.

"Why, Sharlie?" she says into my chest. "I need your grandfather. All night I pray to him. I called him and begged him to take me with him. I don't want this world. Not without him."

I help her to the kitchen table. She balances herself with my arm and takes a seat. She rests her head between the palms of her hands. I get her a glass of water and then return to the stove. I put chorizo in a saucepan and the salty red pork seers in the pan. It only takes a minute to fry and break up the chorizo. I add cooked beans, the juice goes mad in the searing pork, and a droplet of hot bean juice splashes my cheek.

"You're going to burn the tortilla," she says.

I finish cooking the beans and wrap them in a flour tortilla. Monse bites into her burrito. Then she opens her mouth to say something. I shush her with my hand. We eat in silence. Not much to say when you have a mouth full of chorizo.

"Sharlie, you remember when you were thirteen, and I carried you to the shower?" she asks. "You didn't want to shower, so I scooped you up y pa dentro. Think I can still carry you?"

"Nope, I was nine, not thirteen."

"That's right," she says. "Thirteen is when I found you jalandoté la to some dirty magazines."

"Stop lying," I say.

"I'm not lying," she says. "I close my eyes, and it all goes backward, el disco va al reves. That is when you know you're dying. My memories, my youth, my life with Pepper, it's all going in reverse."

"Please, Ma," I say. I don't want to hear it, but her whirlwind of self-loathing comes crashing in.

"Sharlie, I'm dying," she says. "I feel it in my wrists and legs and spine. She rubs her forearms. A pain, arthritic and cold. My bones are soaked in pain. I'm cracking inside. I don't have much longer here. Every time I close my eyes, I see my brothers, tall and handsome. I see you, my little gordito, running around the house with your little huevos hanging out. I see Pepper when he was young, dancing at a fiesta."

She closes her eyes and tilts her head up to the ceiling as if she's receiving a transmission.

"I can see Pepper," she says. "He's in a black suit.

Silver charms dangle along his pant legs, down to his boots. He twirls a lasso into a hoop big enough for the world to step through. He's spinning the hoop around and over himself, whipping it into a frenzy. I can feel Jesus kicking in my belly."

"That's just grief," I say. "We all suffer it."

"This is something else, something stronger than grief. It is acceptance. It knows that death is coming for you."

"Why are you so sad? Didn't Pepper treat you like shit? Didn't he abuse you? What about Jesus? Didn't Pepper hit him time and time again?"

She clinches her fists around the tablecloth.

"I mean, didn't he knock your tooth out and kill your cousin at a wedding?" I dig in. It hurt to talk ill of the dead, but I need Monse out of her depression. I need her alive and strong and angry. I need the woman who told my grade school teacher to fuck off when the teacher said I had dyslexia.

Monse's hands relax. She takes a deep breath, then takes another bite. I want to push the subject but decided to drop it. No need to hurt her when she's already down. She finishes her burrito and then takes the plate over to the sink. On the way back to her seat, she stops before sitting down and whispers into my ear in Spanish.

"Sabes lo que le dijo los cinco dedos a la cara?"

I shake my head no. But before I can figure out

the riddle, she slaps me across the face, knocking the shit out of me. I fall to the floor. She steps on my left ankle and raises her hand like she wants to hit me again. I put my hands up to defend myself.

"Don't you ever talk about your dead grandfather like that! He saved you, and you owe him your miserable mierda life."

She dug her heel into the joint between my foot and ankle until we both heard something pop. I jump to my feet, and a pain jolts up my leg.

"Get out of my house."

I hobbled to the front door and looked back, but Monse had already entered the kitchen.

The Cuero

Some nights, my Grandfather would wake up screaming. He sounded like a banshee, a haunt, la Llorona. The screams echoed down the hall to where Monse and I slept. The screams startled me awake, and I'd tucked deep into the folds of my Grandmother's arms. She'd wake up too, then pat me on the back to calm me.

"Your Abuelo is haunted."

Of course, I could never sleep after that. There's no way my Abeulo is haunted?

Oh, Mexicans, how we love our ghosts; we hold on to them until the day we die. Until we become the ghosts that our progeny hold over their hearts. A Mexica tradition. A conversation with the past. Spoken only in whispers.

According to Monse, Pepper was haunted by his brother, Palacio. Some nights, Palacio came to collect.

For many years, Pepper drank his brother's ghost away. Beer and whiskey work best. Tequila and Mezcal tend to bring out the dead. Now that Pepper had found sobriety, he had no choice but to face his brother standing. Pepper had known the ghost of his brother for a long time now. He went from drinking to praying to God and the Holy Spirit, but his brother kept coming.

My Grandmother also blamed Pepper for Palacio's death. Perhaps that is why when he would wake up screaming his brother's name, she never, not once, went to comfort him. He would call out for her. Shouting her name. She would snuggle me closer and whisper into my ear. "Esta loco."

"Damn, how many people did Pepper kill?" I asked her once. She looked like she wanted to slap me.

As the story goes, Pepper had roused some fat-headed no-good hijo de puta. That man shot Palacio during a scuffle.

Pepper walked into the kitchen one morning and slammed his Luger Single-Six onto the table. The noise made Monse jump, and she spilled some of her coffee on the skillet. The brown juice sizzled and danced into vapor.

"I'm going to ship this gun to Palacio's son."

The proclamation felt grande like Pepper's words echoed through the valley.

I thought about what Pepper had said all day. That night, after I showered and brushed my teeth. After I said my prayers, hail Mary, full of grace, and tucked into bed. Monse held me tight and recited the death of Cuero Arrachera.

Cuero got arrested the night after he shot Palacio in that dusty bar in Aldama. It was by mere chance that Cuero got caught. The police weren't even looking for him, but look, Cuero is trying to jimmy open the door of a '56 coupe just as a patrol car drives by. The two cops watched as Cuero struggled to hook the lock. Cuero grew frustrated with his inability to open the door and slammed his elbow into the window. The window didn't break, but a pain jolted up Cuero's funny bone. He was bandaged from the shoot-out, and his arm throbbed with pain. He kicked the car door and went into a frenzy until his stitches popped open, and he began to bleed.

"They shot you again, Cuero?" The cops laughed. They had him in cuffs and were beating him with leather slappers before he could explain his situation. By the time Cuero had healed up, the judge had ordered to throw Cuero into prison.

Pepper wouldn't shut up about how Cuero would rot in prison. That's all he ever talked about. All it took was warm beer, a watered-down whiskey, and a loose-lipped Pepper would recount the bar fight that got his brother killed.

Then some slag waitress spilled the beans while guzzling down a taco and tequila.

"Yeah, they're letting him out today. His cousin's the bailiff."

Pepper stumbled out of the bar and fumbled for his keys to his brother's car. Pepper drove to the jail, parked by the gates, and waited. A couple of officers passed his car. He waved at them. "I'm waiting for my brother," Pepper said. The cops walked by, ignoring him.

My Grandfather pulled his brother's Luger Six from under the passenger's seat. He would have it. Revenge for his brother. Pepper also pulled his flask from his glove box. He took a long hard swig. Soon after sundown, the gates opened. Pepper pulled the hammer back on the Luger. Three officers walked out. No Cuero. He took a long hard swig. A few hours later, the gates opened again. Two more officers. No Cuero. He finished the flask of whiskey. Then round 'bout midnight, the gates opened, and an officer led Cuero by handcuffs. After releasing Cuero, the jailer spat on the ground.

Pepper was many things, a loving grandfather, a hard-working man, a husband, a drunk, and a born-again Catholic. Still, he lacked sobriety and resolved to shoot Cuero on that night. Pepper's plan seemed simple enough. Walk up to Cuero, shoot him in the chest, and then jump back into the car and drive away, clean into the night. But when Pepper awoke, he saw Cuero standing on the dirt road, staring at him.

Pepper stumbled for the gun, dropping it under his seat. Cuero turned around, heading back for the gates. Not wanting to miss his chance, Pepper turned the key to start the engine. The heavy beast of the car roared. Pepper pulled the car into gear and stomped the gas pedal. The heavy vehicle sprung into action, almost growling as the pistons kicked.

Cuero tried dodging the car, but Pepper swerved into him. Cuero made a loud thud as the coupe's front end smashed into him. The hit sent Cuero flying. He smacked his head against the road.

Pepper slammed the brakes, parked the car, and jumped out. His hands trembled, but he did his best to hold the Luger 6 steady.

"This is for my brother," Pepper shouted.

"Who is your brother?"

At that, Pepper unloaded the gun, firing into Cuero's chest.

I know my Grandfather left Mexico to get a better life. We all like to believe the immigrant myth. They say it keeps the American Dream alive. Work hard, and get a better life. A-okay U.S.A. But my Grandfather had murdered a man in front of a jailhouse. Ain't any way the police could allow that to go unchecked. They hunted him and my Grandmother as far north as Juarez. Then Cuero came out of his coma, and the cops dropped the chase. My Grandfather was no Brazero. No, he crossed that foul line of the border to escape the life he had ruined in Aldama. I suspect many of the other Brazeros were the same way.

As for Cuero, he survived. Spent another three weeks in recovery, but the man lived.

It took a few years to catch word that Cuero had survived. And just like that, an apparition, Palacio, had returned. Hiding in the dark corner of Pepper's mind. Only silenced when Pepper drank himself silly and violent.

Six years later, Pepper heard through the rancho grapevine that the police had arrested Cuero for raping a girl.

It should've been the end. No way the Captain lets him live.

The night Cuero entered the prison, two thick-necked inmates were ordered to shred Cuero to pieces. The Captain wanted him tortured, castrated, and turned to pulp.

The two men crept into Cuero's cell with a key provided by the jailer.

"Wake up, *pendéjo*," whispered Pelón. "Death is here to take you."

Cuero jumped to his feet. He could not make out the men's faces except for their mustaches outlined by the chalky moon.

They closed the cell gate behind them. The screams echoed off the prison's concrete walls and metal bars.

When the two men emerged from the cell, their hands were covered in blood, and their trousers were stained with semen and ass juice. They had turned Cuero inside out, stabbed him, and slit his throat for good measure.

Pelón said something like "for the Captain" or "The Captain sends his regards," as Cuero lay on the floor face down, trying to hold himself in.

"Hey, this *cabrón* doesn't seem to want to die," said Pelón.

"I think we should put a few more *picasos* into

him." Pelón's helper said before walking back into the cell and jamming his knife between Cuero's fifth and sixth rib.

"Culo," gurgled Cuero.

The pain of the blade woke something in Cuero. He came to life with adrenaline and anger, and hate. The pure survival instinct of a madman. He jumped to his feet, knocking the inmate against the wall. Then he slapped Pelón across the side of Pelón's fat head. Pelón lost his balance and went crashing down to the cell floor. Cuero tried pulling the knife from his back but could not reach it. Blood poured from his neck. He removed his shirt, wrapped it around his throat like a scarf, and ran out of his cell and down the hallway with the knife still stuck in his back.

"Run, Cuero, they won't help you!" shouted Pelón.

Cuero reached the guards' booth before collapsing. The guards left him on the floor, groaning and bleeding all night. But he did not die. The following day the lady from the cleaning crew gave him water. Then they dragged him back to the infirmary.

Here's where the story gets a little blurry. According to my Grandmother, Pepper would buy a gun or rifle every six months and mail the weapons and ammo to his nephew, Alan. Alan is Palacio's oldest son. Attached was a note, For Cuero. For all the talk about violence in Mexico, it turns out that buying guns in Mexico is a difficult task, given the people's uprising of 1910. For Pepper, sending guns was a type of remittance, the end of Cuero.

They released Cuero after two years of incarceration. Some say that his bailiff cousin got him off. Others say that Cuero had courted the Captain's daughter and not raped her. The Captain's rage stemmed from Cuero's low-life social status. The Captain's daughter visited Cuero once. After the visit, a group of inmates would attack him. Stringing him up by the neck with a sheet. But Cuero survived. Fortunately, Cuero had a thick, squat neck that some say was unsnapable.

Eventually, the captain got promoted and moved away, taking his daughter.

They released Cuero shortly after. He walked out of the gates, hopeful that his love would be waiting for him. She wasn't.

He walked along the dirt road leading out of *La Pinta* Penitentiary. Twenty-seven miles of cactus and mesquite trees led to the small town of Morrís, Chihuahua.

He walked under the sun for hours. A few cars drove by, but nobody stopped. He watched the sunset into the purple, red, and blue sky. His eyelids weighed heavy. In the quiet moment between sleep and consciousness, his legs marched on while his mind drifted to the constellations he had learned as a boy. Quiche Mayan constellations of turtles, rabbits, and quetzals.

A thin rattle glimmered in the air as he drifted through the stars. It shook him out of his trance and into a boyhood memory of seeing a gray rattlesnake hook itself into the thigh of his caramel-colored dog. The dog yelped and bit at the snake. The snake spun and twirled and faded into the desert brush. Cuero scooped the dog up and ran home. When he got home, the dog's head had swollen, and her tongue was thick and covered in white mucus.

That same sound rattled in Cuero's head, and he jumped to the left. The rattle stopped. Had he created enough distance between himself and the snake? He heard the rattle come up from behind him, and he ran. When he stopped, he could no longer make out the path to Morrís. The desert sun had burnt his face, and his legs were cramping.

But he marched on.

As the sunset turned the sky purple and red, he spotted a large mesquite tree he would rest under. It took him another forty minutes to get to the tree. Perhaps his weary eyes had misjudged the distance. The sun had long faded, and the moon hid behind the clouds. He scanned the area for snakes and coyotes but could not see much in the dark of night. He kicked at the dirt under the tree. He searched for scorpions and niños de la Tierra, fat, pincher-less insects the size of small tarantulas, which he hated.

After clearing the area, Cuero curled up on the ground and pulled his canvas jacket over his head. He drifted into sleep as droplets of rain slapped against his jacket. The Rhythm soothed him, and the cool night air helped his overheated body.

In the morning, he felt a tickle on his cheek, something small crawling around. He wiped his cheek, expecting droplets of rain. Instead, a tiny worm fell off his cheek and onto the ground. The worm wiggled and arched like a dancing grain of white rice. He patted the ground, surprised at how dry it felt. It had rained all night. He touched the scar that itched on his neck and found more maggots. He pushed his head out from under his jacket to find mounds of maggots crawling over him. He jumped to his feet and stomped the jacket on the floor. The larva popped and juiced under his worn shoes.

When he looked up, he saw the horror that had rained on him all night. From the highest limb of the tree hung a man with a bloated gray face, mustached lips, and a stout body not unlike Cuero's. The man had a sign hanging around him that read *thief*. Then Cuero heard a rattle from behind. He scooped up his jacket and headed south at a fast pace. He took it all as a bad omen and traced the sign of the cross onto his head and chest. He walked until he found the road to *Morrís*.

He followed that dusty road until he came upon a dry goods stand. He jingled the few pesos in his pocket. He bought a small chunk of Mennonite cheese and a few corn tortillas.

"I'm traveling through," Cuero said. "Trying to get home. You know of any workaround here?"

"There's a rancho a few miles west," the girl behind the counter answered. "Maybe you can get some work and a bath there."

Cuero thanked her, wolfed down his cheese, and headed west. He came upon a group of men pitchforking hay into a barn.

"I'm looking for work," Cuero said.

The workers nodded towards a man riding a tan horse with a rifle strapped across its rump.

"Boss, I'm traveling through looking for work," Cuero said. "I can work hard and handle a day in the sun."

"Interesting scar," the man on the horse said."Someone cut you?"

"An accident at a rancho," Cuero said. "Got bucked off a horse and landed on a fence. Casi me mato."

Cuero fingered the scar on his neck like a fresh wound. He paused, trying to place the man's angular face, thin lips, and fuzzy eyebrows.

"You a thief?" asked the man on the horse. "We don't take kindly to thieves around here. Lynched us a thief who tried to run off with horses and another man's wife. Maybe you seen him just north of here?"

"No, sir. I'm not a thief," Cuero said. "I didn't see no one. Just trying to make it home, back to Aldáma."

"You from Aldáma? Had family there, once." The man on the horse pulled on the reins until the horse spun around in a tight circle. "You start by loading the hay. The pay ain't much, twenty pesos a week, minus food and lodging."

"Thank you, sir."

"Don't thank me yet. I haven't paid you, and you haven't started working. We'll see how if you have a strong back."

Cuero joined the other men. They worked till sundown moving hay, shoveling manure, and feeding pigs. After sundown, the men went to wash their hands, faces, and necks and gathered in the barn. They each got a bowl of beans and two tortillas.

"At least this food beats the slop from prison," Cuero said.

"You just get out or something?" one of the workers asked.

"No, no," Cuero said. He knew he had made a mistake by flapping his lips. He figured it best to keep quiet.

In the morning, the roosters crowed, and the men got up from hay beds. They washed near the well, pissed behind the barn, and took shits in the holes they dug.

Then they went to work.

On the third day, the boss called for Cuero

"Yes, boss?"

"Some of the workers said you spent some time in La Pinta. This true?"

"No, boss."

"What's your name?"

"Ignacio," Cuero said.

"Don't lie to me, cabron!"

"It's no lie, boss. On my mother's grave. "I'm just a worker trying to get home."

"You're just a worker, but twenty-seven years ago, you were in a bar in Aldáma."

"No, boss, you got the wrong man."

Cuero spun around and started running. His legs were bags of concrete. No matter how hard he pushed, he could not run fast enough. He heard the snake's rattle from behind him.

"Don't," Cuero yelled.

He heard the hammer of a rifle click back and knew this would be his end. The rest of eternity in the dirt, being eaten by worms.

Then two blasts cut through the air, and Cuero crumbled onto the ground.

The workers ran out of the barn. They saw Cuero on the ground. The boss reloaded his rifle and unloaded it into Cuero's back. He loaded his gun again and emptied the gun, shooting until Cuero turned to pulp. When he ran out of bullets, he swung and slammed the butt of the rifle against the back of Cuero's skull. Then the boss pulled his revolver and shot at the pile of meat on the ground until his gun emptied. Then he took the pistol and whipped Cuero into soggy peaks of flesh.

"Why, Jefe? Why?" One of the workers came from behind and hugged the boss. "Please stop! Please!"

The boss shrugged him off and stomped on the mess of flesh before him.

"This mierda killed my father."

"I thought the man we lynched two weeks ago had killed your father," said the worker.

"Guess not," said the boss. "My father put five bullets into this piece of shit, and he didn't die. My uncle shot him in the chest. He didn't die. Two men in prison slit his throat and stabbed him, and the fucker still didn't die. I need to make sure this pedazo de mierda is dead. Bring me the rifle."

The workers rushed to the boss's horse and returned with a bolt-action Remington. The boss unloaded the rifle into the stain of Cuero's crushed skull.

"Palacio's son, Alan, killed Cuero," Monse said. "Pepper bought him those guns because Pepper knew his nephew had huevos de fierro."

"Do I have huevos de fiero?"

"No," Monse said. "You don't." Then she poked at my thighs and tickled my ribs.

Chile Colorado

While I grate Munster cheese at the table. My grandmother stands over a greased pan stirring chile de Arbol, potatoes, and meat. The chile stings my nose, and I sneeze over the pan de huevo at the center of the kitchen table.

"Salud," says my grandmother.

Her once-full cheeks now sag on her bones. My grandfather's death has deflated her like an old tire. The dark circles around her eyes are gray with wrinkles, and her hair fades into thin silver slivers. She still hasn't found her dentures.

I ask her about my uncle, Jesus. I ask when he's coming and if he's bringing his wife. She's too busy cooking over the hot stove. Her movements are short and brutish, but they are heavily seasoned with the precision of a person that has cooked their entire life. How many burritos? She asks.

She rolls up two burritos for me and one for her.

She bites into the burrito with her back molars. They are the last four teeth in her skull. Then she unrolls her burrito and scoops up the meat and potatoes with a piece of her flour tortilla. "It's easier this way," she says in Spanish, then shovels the food into her mouth.

I ask her about her dentures.

"I've looked everywhere, under the bed, behind the couch. I even looked in my Viejo's room," she says with a mouth full of semi-chewed food.

Of course, her eyes gloss over. Anytime she mentions my grandfather, she wants to cry. She's about to remind me of the hardships of widowhood. This time I put my arm around her shoulders because I'm not a fucking bastard. I don't want to push her away while she is in grief. We can get her new dentures.

"Your grandfather knocked out the first tooth," she says, giving me half a smile.

I knew he abused her, but I never witnessed it myself. Though his abuse of my Grandmother stopped before I was born, Monse had told me the stories of my Abuelo, the world-class asshole.

"I miss him so much," she says. "He was a bastard, but I loved him." She leans her head on me.

"We all miss him," I say. "But you have to stop."

"Don't think I can," she says. "I need to be with Braulio."

For an instant, as brief as the flutter of a fly, I thought maybe it would be better if she were a pile of ashes in an urn next to the leather box containing Pepper's ashes.

"I know you love him, but come on. He knocked out your teeth. How can you love someone that caused you so much pain?"

She cries into my shoulder. I tell her she needs to get out, even if it's to church. "You can't spend all day in this house waiting to die."

She wipes her tears when she hears Jesus's truck pull into the driveway. We wait in silence until Jesus enters the house. My arm is still around her shoulder. Jesus walks in, and he's all smiles. He kisses Monse on the cheek and then leans over to hug and kiss me.

"Damn, Charlie, you smell like a hangover," Jesus says. "You go out last night?"

"Nope, stayed at home."

He turns his head to the stove and nods toward it. Monse struggles to get up and wobbles over to the stove.

She asks if I want another burrito, but I'm full.

"I want two," Jesus says.

Jesus plops on the couch in the living room and turns on the Raider's game. Monse takes him a plate of burritos and some napkins. She stands over him, holding the plate for Jesus until the Raiders end their play. Then she hands him the plate. Jesus takes the plate while cussing out the ref for miscalling the play.

Jesus and my grandmother share the same dumpling body, thick ankles, broad back, and no ass. They both have light skin and curly hair. I look like my grandfather, with copper-colored skin, a barrel chest, and bird legs.

"Aye, my leg hurts," Monse says as she limps back

to the kitchen.

Jesus tells her to sit and tells her she needs to rest. Then he asks her to bring him a soda. What a fat lazy bitch. I help Monse sit and get a can of apple soda from the fridge. Like Monse, I stand before Jesus and wait till the play ends.

"Goddamn Raiders!" Shouts Jesus. He snatches the soda from my hand. I go back to the kitchen table and sit with Monse. She has a stack of letters in front of her that she wants me to translate for her. One of the letters demands payment for the services rendered during my grandfather's funeral. They want $2067.42.

"I thought all of Pepper's funeral expenses were paid?" I say loud enough for Jesus to hear me.

"I gave everything to Jesus," Monse says. He paid all the bills.

"Yo, Jesus, this bill says we still owe for Pepper's funeral."

I wave the envelope in the air to show him the bill. Jesus focuses on the game, then stuffs the burrito into his mouth. Red chile spills out the back end of the burrito.

"Quit bothering me, he says between chews. I'm trying to watch the fucking game, and you're here all bull-shitting."

Mom got a bill for the funeral, güey. Says she owes money. But he's not listening to me. He's pretending to be into the game, but the game's on a commercial break. I walk over to him and show him the letter. He looks up from eating, snatches the letter from my hand, and glances over it before dropping it on the couch beside him. The game starts again.

"Even with all the money gathered and the insurance, we're still short, he says. I put in some cash from my own pocket." He points to the T.V., indicating the game has started.

"What about the money from the Meat Packers Union? The money Williams put together?"

"The union only put up a couple hundred bucks," Jesus says. "Didn't even cover the cost of the food at the funeral. Besides, she'll be okay with Pepper's pension and social security. The house is already paid for."

"Williams said the Union gathered six thousand for Pepper."

"Hey, Dick-face Tracy," he says. "Quit asking stupid questions and watch the fucking game. Besides, you know how mayates are. Williams probably stole it." Jesus shoves the other half of the burrito into his mouth and lays the plate on the floor.

"Don't fight," Monse says, please. She gets up and limps to the stove to make another burrito for Jesus.

"Sharlie, bring me your tío's plate?"

Jesus slides the red chile-splattered plate across the tile with his foot.

"And bring me another Manzana soda, Charlie."

I bend over to pick up the plate. Jesus jumps to his feet and yells. "Touchdown! Touchdown! Raider-nation, bitch."

I return with his food.

"Williams wouldn't lie," I say.

"He's a fucking nigger. That's why he lied," Jesus says. "You know what? I'm fucking out of here. I don't need to be questioned about what some fucking jungle monkey told you." He stands up and stares me down. He has about sixty pounds on me, and his eyes are fury.

Monse rushes into the room and stands between us. My heart jumps up to my throat. If Monse hadn't run in, he would have swung at me.

Monse's begging him to stay, but he says he has to leave because he can't enjoy the game with my questioning. He storms out of the house and speeds off in his truck.

Monse's at the door, making the sign of the cross. She turns to me and says, "he's your uncle. You need to have more respect."

I tell her I'm just looking out for her.

"He's my blood, Sharlie," she says. "Remember that."

I've become a stranger, an unwanted visitor. This place no longer feels like home, not without Pepper, and for the first time in my life, I feel what it means to be a bastard.

I don't return to Monse's house or call her for almost two months, not even during Christmas. When I finally return, she asks me for forgiveness. I forgive her and promise her that nothing has changed, but everything has changed.

We All have Needs, Pepper.

My Grandmother never said anything decent about my mother, Mercy. *She's a puta, she's a drogadicta, she never loved you.* That was all I ever heard about my mother. I once asked Monse if she had my mother's contact information. I got slapped in the mouth. One of the few times Monse had ever hit me.

Then one day, five months after her husband had died, my Grandmother admitted that she regretted what she had done to my mom, Mercy.

"It started when your grandfather came home too drunk, speaking nonsense, a mess of English and Spanish. Every word was a sloppy slur layered over another sloppy insult. He stumbled into the kitchen, one knight, and in his whirlwind of words, he told me that Mary, his chapete was pregnant.

I tried to kick him out of the house. When he would not leave, I ran at him and clawed his shoulders and neck. The cabron fell over, laughing. I kicked him and slapped his head, but he kept laughing. I struck him that the palms of my hands turned red and sore. My toes ached from kicking his ribs.

'Get out,' I screamed, and you know what the Hijo de puta said? He told me that If I left him, I would be nothing. I would have nothing. He called me a vale vergas."

Monse looked at me. Her eyes were glossy from the tears.

"I never had a job, never learned to drive, barely learned English."

If she had to work, who would care for their son? Who would pick him up from school, pack his bologna sandwiches, and tuck him in at night? Too proud for food stamps, too Mexican for welfare.

Monse wiped her nose and tears. She looked at me, her eyes lost on the picture of the Virgin Mary behind me.

"Have you seen my teeth?" She said without looking at me.

"I'll help you find them."

"Let me tell you something, Sharlie. If Pepper had not felt so guilty about my cousin dying, he would have left Jesus and me. Mary wasn't like his other chapetes; she wasn't some cheap drunk whore. I think he really loved her. Maybe more than Pepper loved me. That's why Pepper brought you in and adopted you. He recognized himself in you. The same Indio face and dark skin. He left one of his family in Aguas Calientes. And not one time has he ever bothered to call them or visit them. Poof, gone just like that. One of his sons tracked us down once when living in Juarez. Pepper ran that poor boy out into the streets. If Mary had given birth to a son instead of your mother, Pepper might have left me for good. But your grandmother lacked the strength to carry a man. I doubt she could even take a good sock to the jaw."

After the birth of my mother, Pepper did not abandon Mary. He lived with them, taking care of my newborn mother.

My uncle, Jesus, told me Monse tried to hide Pepper's absence. Monse and Pepper came up with a lie, Pepper had found a job wrangling horses.

Pepper wasn't around much in those days. But when he came around, Pepper told Jesus these wild stories about a beastly mare that no man could tame. It took eight men to keep her from jumping over the corral and running back to the wild.

As Pepper spun his story, Monse refried beans and eggs, trying her best not to cry but splashing the eggs in hot grease with her tears. Sizzle and pop. Her husband had become her accomplice.

"The food at the rancho is terrible, *mijo*," said Pepper. "Nothing but beans with no salt and old crusty bread. Not like your Mom's delicious food."

"What happened to the horse?" Jesus asked.

"Esperate," said Pepper. "Let me get some food in my stomach."

Pepper shoveled a scoop of beans and eggs into his mouth, covering his mustache in yoke and crumbs.

"El Jefe asked me to break a mare," said Pepper. "I walked up to that beast and stared into her eyes. They were so black and deep, like staring into an abyss.

Yo soy el Chingon, I said to myself. I grabbed her mane and shook her massive head. God, was she beautiful and strong. She moved in tight circles, kicking up dust and dirt. I jumped up to my feet and took hold of her mane once again. This time, the men held tight onto the ropes. I pulled on her hair and swung around until I got on her back. She bucked and kicked, screaming these horrible horse screams. Then, after about ten minutes, she calmed. The men removed the ropes around her neck, and she remained calm. I walked her over to the hay, and I realized my mistake. She tricked me."

Pepper and Jesus shoveled beans into their mouths, wiped their lips, and drank from their glasses of milk. Jesus's eyes were so wide they could pop.

"Tell me more, Dad."

"I felt her muscles tense as she jumped into the air. I held on as tight as I could. She jumped into the post smashing my ribs, but I held strong. Then she jumped into the air and rolled over, crashing her weight down on me. I pulled her mane hard as I could, then she jumped, rolled over a few times, and returned to her feet. We continued like that for six hours, no, for six days. Fighting day and night. By the second day, I could no longer feel my hands. By the third, we were both breathing heavy. I grabbed her left ear and drew her head to my lips. Yo te voy acavar! Then I spat on her face. She kicked and bucked so hard that it sounded like thunder cracked the sky. The other men feared she would bring the barn down. She bucked and snarled and rolled on the floor. I tied a rope around her neck and my hand in case my grip gave. We were both exhausted, red-eyed, and dehydrated by the fourth day. But let me tell you a secret, Mijo, horses can't sweat. Their bodies get overheated, they start to pant, and they let their tongues drop from their jaws. That's when I saw my chance. I grabbed her raspy tongue and tied a knot around it. I pulled so hard I almost yanked that dry tongue out of her skull. She yelped and fought and bucked, but every time she kicked, I yanked on that fucking tongue till, finally, she dropped down to her knees. I slowly got off her and walked around to the front. I untied the rope and singled to the other Caballeros to bring water. To this day, Mijo, I'm the only one to ride La Negra Soledad."

"You think I could ride La Negra Soledad?" Jesus asked.

"No, Mijo, your mom has made you soft."

Then as Monse was about to sit down, Pepper and Jesus lifted their plates and asked for more huevos.

"And that's how we lived," Monse said. "Then the murder happened."

Markito

The plan seemed simple enough. Pepper would drive his family down to Aldama for a wedding. He could suggest to his wife that she and their son stay behind for a couple of weeks. He could point out that their son was getting soft living in the United States. He could promise to return in a couple of weeks. He told her that she needed to spend time with her family. As the list of reasons to stay in Mexico grew, so did his ambition to start a new life with Mary and his baby daughter, Mercy.

In the weeks leading up to the wedding, Pepper had, for the first time, maybe in his entire life, treated Monse and Jesus with some love and respect. He stopped going to *Gordita's* and drank his beers at home. He would even pour Monse a glass, and they would toast to her cousin's matrimony.

Monse loved her cousin, Markito, from the day he was born. She watched as her aunt Lencha breached and eventually gave birth in the bedroom. Watching a birth did not shock Monse. She had seen, time and again, cows, goats, and pigs give birth. The creation of life went hand in hand with life in *el rancho*. Markito had been a breached birth, and Monse marveled as the nurse, elbow deep into Lencha, had managed to pull out little Markito. After the nurse had cut the umbilical cord, she tasked Monse with burying the placenta under a tree. "Make sure you pick a tree far away from the livestock because sometimes the coyotes can smell it." The nurse said as she handed Monse a bowl of gooey placenta. Monse buried the placenta at the base of a mesquite tree near the creek.

You can imagine Monse's joy when she heard Markito's voice over the telephone. Markito was getting married.

Pepper tried his best to fill the car joyfully on the drive down to Aldama. He told Jesus about the ranches and the beautiful, strong horses. He promised Jesus that they would ride the horses down to the creek, and if they were lucky, they would spot and shoot a coyote. Jesus jumped around with excitement in the back seat. They even stopped in the desert to practice shooting with Pepper's Ruger Single-Six .22.

On the ride to Aldama, Monse sat quietly, watching the desert zoom past the car window. She knew Pepper would leave them in Mexico, just like he had left his other families. For the entire five-hour drive, she did not utter a single word.

Pepper promised his son that the star-filled nights in Mexico would be so marvelous that Jesus would think he was dreaming.

On the morning of the wedding, Pepper sat the edge of the bed and lit a can of shoe polish wax on fire. He watched as the flame danced on top of the can and let out streams of black smoke. At that moment, Jesus walked by and saw the fire coming from the shoe polish and gave his dad a smile.

"Bring me your boots, mijo," Pepper said.

Pepper polished Jesus's boots and thought about his son's life in Mexico. He tried convincing himself that his son's stay in Mexico would make him a strong man Pepper could respect. A strong Mexican with a strong work ethic. He may not see Jesus for a very long time.

The two sat on the edge of the bed. Jesus watched as his father rubbed the hot wax onto the brown calf-skin boot. The wax cooled into a yellow film. "Here is the right way to polish a boot: start by cleaning the boot of any debris, put some heat on the wax so it melts, rub it into the boot, and then buffer away," Pepper said. "You see? Like that."

Pepper snapped the buffer cloth over the toe of Jesus's boot. "When I was your age, Mijo, my family didn't have anything." Pepper continued to work the cloth over the leather boot. "Sometimes, the only way we could feed each other was to work shining shoes. My brother, Palacio, and I would set up in front of the capital or at the police station, and we would shine shoes so shiny you could see your reflection in the shoes. One day I saw you standing in the reflection, and I knew I would have a strong and handsome son."

Jesus smiled, and his cheeks turned rosy. He wanted to cry, but he knew that would break the moment he and his father were having. His father hated to see Jesus cry. So instead, Jesus sucked in his tears and thanked his father for the shoeshine.

Pepper pulled his gray vaquero sports coat over his shoulders. He gave himself one final look in the mirror, twirled his thick mustache, and then put his cowboy hat on. By this time tomorrow, he would be back in the States. Holding Mary and Mercy. He took a deep breath, smiled a toothy grin, holstered Remington Single-Six, and went off to meet his family before heading to the wedding.

All the weddings in Aldama were held in the town square. People poured out of the church and into the party. They had slaughtered a pig, and there was enough mezcal and beer to last for several parties. At first, Pepper drank at a slow pace. He didn't want the dreaded cruda looming over him while driving to the States. The last thing he needed was a bad hangover pulling at his stomach and head while his heart filled with the guilt of leaving his family behind. Was it a well-thought-out plan? No. But Pepper was never one for well-laid plans.

Then the groom, Markito, bumped into Pepper on the dance floor. They were both all smiles and hugs. Markito called his friends over, and they came stumbling through the crowd holding a bottle of mezcal up in the air. "Pa'rriba, pa'bajo, pa'centro, pa'dentro." The mezcal burned its way down Pepper's throat. He needed a beer to chase away the hot alcohol. Then another beer to keep up the good spirits. The band played all night. Jesus was off playing with his cousins.

As Pepper danced with Monse, he noticed the sweat glistening off her forehead and the soft glow of the tin-can lights reflected off her cheeks. Pepper saw her beauty for the first time in a long time. He strolled through his mind's memory remembering how he had first fallen in love with her. Monse's father hated Pepper and even tried to kill him twice. But his love for her could easily overcome her family's jealousy. He decided to make love to his wife before returning to the U.S.

At midnight the church bells rang across the town of Aldama, and everyone cheered at the end of the twelfth bell. They raised their pistols into the air and fired away. A salute to the newlywed bride and groom. The world had blurred, and Pepper could hardly stand by this point. He reached for his holstered Single-six. The gun felt heavy and cold in his hand as he walked through the crowd looking for Monse.

Markito held his gun up in the air, and the crowd around him cheered. Monse reached over and gave her cousin a kiss on the cheek. Everyone cheered, including Pepper. It was customary in Aldama to fire your guns in the air during a celebration.

Markito shot first. After all, this was his wedding. The sound startled Pepper sober. He aimed his gun into the air and fired all six rounds, then gave out the loudest grito he had ever given. He turned to look over at Monse. Her face was covered in blood, and she was doing everything she could to hold up her cousin, Markito. Then Pepper realized that the ear-piercing grito he thought he had yelled out was, in fact, the sound of Monse and Markito's wife screaming.

Pepper was so drunk that when he aimed his gun up into the air, he sloppily aimed it to the side. His limp wrist turned at the recoil, and he fired two more shots.

The ringer in his ears drowned out any other sound. As his hearing came back, he heard loud cries and screams.

One of the shots hit Markito in the face just below his left eye.

The adrenaline rushed through Peppe's body, and his pupils contracted at the horror of seeing the blood gushing out of Markito's face. Maru was screaming in agony as she had been shot. She looked up at Pepper, her eyes burning with pure hatred, and reached for Markito's gun, which had fallen next to his body. Pepper froze with fear as she aimed the gun at him. She pulled the trigger, and the hammer clicked, but the gun did not fire. She pulled the trigger again and again. All six chambers were empty. The screams of the crowd snapped Pepper out of his temporary freeze. He had to leave, to run away from the horror of Markito bleeding out on the ground.

He liked Markito and loved his family. How could he have? Oh God, no.

As he ran out of the town square, he heard Monse's family screaming and crying. Bullets zipped past him. His legs pumped harder and harder with adrenaline. Until he reached his canary yellow Maverick. He threw up before jumping into the car seat. The Mezcal burned twice as much on the way out as it did going down. He slammed the transmission into drive and floored the gas pedal. Into the dusty night, Pepper drove away.

This Abuela Has Fangs

"Una ves," my grandmother said. Your grandfather pulled up to the house at four in the morning, then cut his car's engine and swayed back and forth. He opened the door and vomited. Then he stumbled to his bedroom, unclipped his leather belt buckle, pulled off his boots, then fell onto the red-felt blanket covering his bed.

He woke to find me standing over him. I shook his shoulders back and forth, trying to wake him. He rolled over and pushed me away with his palm. He was covered in vomit.

"Stop, Vieja," he mumbled.

"It's six, estas late."

He got to his feet, his head heavy. His breath smelled like tripe pickled in tequila. He jumped into the cold shower, rinsed himself, and jumped out. He dressed while still wet. In a hurry, he sped through the house and got his thermos of coffee and a brown bag with two egg burritos. His work clothes and construction boots bounced around in the back seat as he sped down I-10.

When he punched in, the time card read 6:35 in bright red.

"You're late, Pepper," the plant manager said.

"Sorry, boss, a hundred times sorry," Pepper said. It won't happen again.

"Best not happen again," the plant manager said. "Or I'll move your ass to the third shift."

Nobody wanted the third shift. It ran all night, hauling and cleaning pork that stank something rancid. No one stayed at Payton for too long if they worked the third shift.

Pepper unloaded the first truck in forty-two minutes. After the first truck, he took a ten-minute break to shit and wash his mouth. By the time he got back, another truck had pulled up for unloading.

"Get a move on, man," the greasy trucker yelled at Pepper, "Andale."

When Pepper opened the back of the truck, the smell of the cow carcasses smacked Pepper across the face. The stench of the halved cows pulled at his intestines until he threw up.

"This meat's gone bad," Pepper said.

"You gonna stand around all day? You aren't getting paid to puke."

Pepper's stomach coiled and tensed.

"What the shit?" The trucker said. "You'll have to hold your lunch, or I'll talk to the boss. Get yourself together beaner."

Pepper wiped the bile from his mustache. The inside of his head pounded.

"Don't mess with my job, or you and I will have

a problem."

The trucker's face turned split-beet red. "You wanna go, spic?" He thrust his belly into Pepper's chest.

Pepper put up his dukes, cocked a fist back, and swung. His fist landed between the trucker's second and third chin. But the trucker was unfazed. The trucker laughed, grabbed Pepper by the white smock, and head-butted his left eye. Pepper's eye swelled, and his legs noodled. His stomach coiled and released a spew of scrambled eggs, flour tortillas, coffee, and bile. The trucker took a whiff, hunched over, and puked, too.

Pepper punched the trucker in the ear, then smashed another fist into the trucker's neck. The trucker put his beefy hand up to defend himself. "No mas, please no mas," the trucker said before vomiting.

We're even gringo. Clean yourself up, and I'll get you a smock to change into.

Pepper unloaded the rancid meat while the trucker cleaned himself off with a hose.

It was the most exhausting shift in Pepper's life. His body ached. He was a sore bruise. Every few hours, he puked or dropped a hot mess of diarrhea.

Pepper pulled up to his house and honked the car horn. His son, Jesus, to move out of the way.

"Hey, Pops!"

Pepper didn't want Jesus to see the fat purple bruise on his left eye. He slithered into his house, moving fast and quiet. When Monse saw the purple pulp eye, she was all over him with questions. What happened to your eye? The air sat heavy with the smell and sizzle of onions and searing liver. Pepper's head was pounding from the heavy-fisted knuckles of the truck driver. The smell of the liver and onions made him lick his chops like a cartoon wolf. Monse turned back to the stove. Pepper crept up behind her and placed his hands on her waist. He thrust his hips into her backside and kissed her on the nape of her neck. Monse shooed him away with the spatula.

"I got into it with a gordo from work," Pepper said. "Pero me lo chinge."

Monse plated the fried liver and onions in front of Pepper. She sprinkled the dish with cilantro.

How many tortillas? She asked.

Pepper spooned chile de arbol salsa over the liver and asked for four tortillas. She sat next to him while he shoveled the liver into his mouth. He finished every last morsel of the liver. She wanted to talk to him, but he was ravenous and kept pointing at his food every time she asked a question. He used the last bits of his corn tortilla to wipe all the juices and chile from the plate and shoved it into his mouth. Monse got up to serve him more, but he grabbed her wrist when she reached for his plate. He unzipped his pants, letting his belly loose and exposing part of his member to her. She smacked his hand away, and he tucked himself back in. "That's for later," he said.

She offered him a donut from a greasy paper bag. Then she took his plate and placed it in the sink. She found a Pumada de La Campana tin in the medicine drawer, a cream used for rashes, bruises, burns, pimples, eczema, and the evil eye.

She dabbed Pepper's face. The warmth of her fingers soothed his swollen eye. Her hands were gentle as she rubbed the pomade over his bruise. Her motions soothed him into a state between sleep and being awake. She continued to work his eye like a cut man hunched over a boxer.

Jesus ran into the house, all excited. Mama, is the food ready?

He washed his hands, sniffed at the air, and sat at the table, wiggling his hips. He asked Pepper about his eye. Pepper sat there, half hunched over and snoring. The plate of food, Monse placed in front of Jesus looked so good that Jesus's eyes opened wide. He got to work chomping on the fried liver and onions. Jesus's hand moved across the table towards the donut bag and pulled a glazed donut. He pushed his finger into the soft dough, then pulled it out and licked it.

"You have to eat it now," Pepper said.

Jesus laughed, kicking his legs back and forth. Then sat the donut next to his plate of liver and onions. He scarfed the food down and then asked for more. Monse took his plate and warmed some tortillas on the comal. Then Jesus scooted his chair next to his dad.

"I kicked this big fat white guy's ass at work today," Pepper said. "He got one lucky shot, but after that, *me lo chinge*."

"Why'd you get in a fight?" Jesus asked.

"Look, son, you never let anyone talk down to you, Pepper said. Not if they're white or Mexican and especially not a negro. If they do, you kick them right in the huevos, and bam!"

Jesus laughed and went to hug Pepper, but before they could embrace, Jesus pushed his finger into the plum bruise of Pepper's eye. The pain, an electric charge searing his nerves, shot from Pepper's eye down into his tailbone. Pepper yelped and jumped up from his chair. Jesus jumped off the chair and ran to Monse. Pepper touched his eye, careful not to shoot another pain through his body like Jesus' chubby finger poke. Pepper looked at the donut with the big dent from Jesus's busy fingers. "Pínche Gordo!"

Pepper lunged at Jesus, grabbed him by the chubby arm, and slapped the shit out of Jesus. Literally, Jesus farted from the fright of the slap. The boy's cheek turned red, and he cried out.

"You want to be a crybaby, cabrón?" Pepper pulled his belt from his waist.

Monse jammed herself between the two of them, ready to stop Pepper. She wrapped her arms around him, then lifted him off the floor.

"Run, Gordo!" she shouted. "Lock yourself in the room."

Pepper's legs kicked back, trying to wiggle out of her grip.

"Pasiguate!" She yelled. "Cálmate."

Monse's voice sent a fright into his chest, a whirlwind of shame from feeling so helpless against her. He stopped fighting, stopped twitching, and then took a deep breath. Monse had misjudged his temperament. When she let go, he smashed his fist into her mouth. His movement was fast and well-calculated. She felt every knuckle crashing into her mouth. The blow snapped her head back, and then she fell to her knees.

Her head rang, and she felt something shift in her mouth, hard like a pebble. He bent over to pick up his belt from the floor. She cupped her mouth, trying to hold the blood in. Tremor rumbled in her gut and worked its way into her hands. She knelt in front of my Grandfather, crying.

Seeing his wife so weak only made him angrier and stronger. He could smell her iron-rich blood. He could feel her trembling. He was a dog in how violently he attacked her, swinging his belt down, pounding, and yelling at her. All the while getting more excited with every welt.

She heard the leather smack against her skin before she felt the sting. She cried out for Pepper to stop. Her cries drove him mad with blood lust, and he swang harder. After the fourth strike, all went silent. She calmed her heart in her pain. Her ideas were fueled by anger. She thought of Pepper shooting her cousin. She remembered when he tried to abandon her. She thought back to Pepper smacking their son. A fury grew in Monse, hatred for her Pepper like she's never felt. In that pain, she formed a mantra, *Me la vas a pagar. Me la vas a pagar. Me la vas a pagar.* When she stopped crying, he was taken aback.

"Pinche Gorda!" he said. Then he stormed off.

She stayed on the floor momentarily, trying her best to gather herself. At that moment, she decided to never cry in front of her husband. He had hurt her bad. Her mouth pulsed with pain, and blood pooled in the palm of her hand. Something heavy and hard swam around in the blood.

Pepper returned to the kitchen. Concerned about what he had done, he picked up Monse off the floor.

"I'm sorry, Vieja," he said. "I just got so mad because that fucking gordo hit my bruise." He brushed her thick curls out of her face.

Her lips and chin were stained with blood. She opened her hands and lifted her palms toward his face. In the little pool of blood sat her front tooth. A yellow kernel with roots swimming in blood.

Pepper's Truck

At this point, visiting my grandmother felt more like a chore than a longing desire to see her. She called me earlier and promised to tell me about my mother. I had begged and begged my grandmother to tell me about my mother all my life. She always held it over me. Sometimes, she shared little insights. I had pieced together most of my mom's history through this patchwork of story fragments.

My mom got pregnant at fifteen and abandoned me six months after. Monse calls her a drogaddicta, but I never found out what she was addicted to.

So I waited a while before I got to Monse's house. She smiles a big toothless smile. "Sit, sit," she tells me. Her mouth puckers up when she talks. "I've been cooking all day. I made enchiladas, your favorite."

I wouldn't say I like enchiladas, not red ones, but I pretend to be excited and hungry. "Gracias."

The red chile stains her upper lip and wispy silver mustache as we eat. "I noticed you had to jump-start your truck last time, Monse says. Where'd you buy it? A junkyard?"

"It beats the bus."

"Sell that basura and take your grandfather's truck instead. I don't want it here anyways."

"I can't take his truck."

She walks to the living room window and pushes the curtain back, revealing the black truck sagging in the driveway. The paint is faded, and rust has gathered around the tire walls.

"Can't take it," I say. "Can't afford the maintenance."

She looks me straight in the eyes and says, "It's the last thing I have of him. And the bank wants to take it."

"Let them."

She squints her eyes, "you owe me for taking you in," she tells me. "God knows how you would've turned out if you'd stayed with your mother. You might not even be alive today. Tossed in the dumpster como un pedaso de basura. Is that what you would've wanted?"

I don't want to hear any of this. I get up to leave. Fuck this guilt trip. Monse gets up and shuffles over to the front door, blocking it.

"Is this what you want to talk about? My mom? Because I've heard this from you before. I've heard all the stories about how you saved my life and how I would be nothing without you. Well, guess what?"

She laughs a loud cackle of a laugh.

"I'm a fucking cook, and I like drugs and beer. I turned out to be what you promised to have saved me from. I've done it all, passes, mota, hongos, acid, ecstasy, all of it, just like my mom.

She looked at me with a glare straight from hell. "Well, what do you want me to tell you? That your mom was a puta? Que todos se la cochaban. That she would have sold you for crack. That you were born addicted. That we had to take you to special doctors to save you. You're a little slow, tonto, because your mom smoked and drank when she was pregnant with you."

I needed to get out of Monse's house. She had worked some voodoo mind shit on me, and I needed out. But she stood tall and firm at the door. So I did the cowardly thing and went for the back. She ran over and pushed the door shut before I could get out.

"Don't go, *Sharlie*," she says. "Soon, I'll be next to your grandfather, a box of ashes on some shelf."

I wait for her to say something else, but she looks at the floor. Her eyes filled with tears.

"I'll take the truck," I say.

She doesn't say anything and goes catatonic. I let go of the door handle. She reaches into her chile-stained apron and hands me my grandfather's keys.

The inside of the truck still smells like my grandfather's anise-scented cologne. The truck doesn't turn over. I think about jump-starting it with my little ranger, but what do I know about engines and car repair?

When I go back inside, Monse has her head in her hands, and she's crying. I think about comforting her.

Instead, I throw the keys onto the couch and split.

Mercy in High School

An oxidized copper statue of General John J. "Black Jack" Pershing stood at the entrance, pointing into the air, charging forward, forever in the history books, searching for the elusive Pancho Villa.

Despite being late for class, Mercy stopped to stare into the statue's flaring nostrils and cooper irises. A thought grew. She had seen this look on the faces of principals and police officers and had even seen the look on her social studies teacher, Mrs. Witmore, a balding fat bitch with a pink complexion and green eyes.

The bell rang three times. Mercy was late for class

Mercy couldn't afford another visit to the principal's office. She got in trouble last week for fighting, and the principal needed one good reason to expel her from school.

She sprinted to class, flying by classrooms and hall monitors. "Slow down, young lady."

Mercy got to Mrs. Witmore's class out of breath and covered in sweat.

"Mercy, you're always late," Mrs. Witmore said.

Mercy explained that she had to drop her sister off at school.

"I'm not concerned with your excuses or lies, Mercy. Your responsibility is to be in class on time and ready to learn. Do you understand?"

Mercy sat down at her desk.

"No, ma'am, you come here." Mrs. Witmore pulled a red slip from her desk and bent over to write on it. Her gut popped the bottom button of her blouse open.

"Your button," Mercy said while pointing down at Mrs. Witmores stomach.

"What? What did you say to me? What was that?"

Mrs. Witmore turned all shades of rouge.

She wanted to eat Mercy.

"Your shirt," Mercy said. "The button's undone." The entire class giggled.

"Get to the goddamn office now!" Mrs. Witmore growled.

There it is, thought Mercy, that same fucking look as that fucking statue.

Instead of walking to the Principal's office, Mercy detoured into the restroom. Her eyes watered from the ammonia cutting through the air. She sat in the blue stall and chewed on her nails, and then she pulled out her composition book and wrote down the sentence, fuck that gringa bitch, Mrs. Witmore. The class bell rang, and Mercy shot out of the stall. She waited in the hallway for her friends, Santana and Lupita. They always skipped their third period together. Usually, they'd end up at Album Park until the end of third period and lunch.

At Album Park, they sat under a Nogal and smoked grass. Santana played his guitar, struggling through the chords and harmonies of Sunny and the Sunliners. Sometimes Lupita accompanied him.

"Dude," Santana said. "I heard Mrs. Witmore gave it to you in social studies."

"You know how it is? That perra hates me ever since I asked her how Columbus could've discovered the Americas if people were already living here?"

"Yeah, that's one kooky lady," Lupita said. She needs to be more down with the Raza."

"She wants to keep us down," Santana said.

"I know where she lives. We could T.P. her house or something." Mercy said.

Santana laughed and strummed the chords to *Brown Eyed Girl.* He sang the song to Mercy, but she knew better and didn't pay him too much attention. Besides, Santana and Lupita were kinda a thing.

I got to pick up my sister, Mercy said. She stood up and walked away before her friends could protest.

Mercy walked down Bentencourt until she came across East Elementary. She spotted her sister, Marisol, sitting in a swing, kicking her legs back and forth. She called out to Marisol, but her sister ignored her and swung faster and faster. Then Marisol flew through the air. The plastic ligas holding her ponytail caught the desert sun and prismed into a thousand rainbows.

Marisol fell to the ground. Mercy ran to her, and so did the teacher, Mrs. Saucedo.

"I thought your mom was picking Marisol?" Mrs. Saucedo asked.

"Not today. I got out of class early."

Mrs. Saucedo placed her hand on Mercy's shoulder. Mrs. Saucedo was the type of woman Mercy wished her mom could be. Mrs. Saucedo was round and soft. She smelled clean, like flour, and always felt warm, unlike Mercy's mom's raw meat and boozy smell.

Back home, two eggs sizzled over a frying pan, their yokes still soft. Mercy stabbed at the yolks until the yellow bled out over the whites. She shook the pan and sprinkled garlic salt, and pepper over the eggs before stirring them. They thickened into yellow clouds.

She heard the wrought-iron screen door squeak open and the wood door banging against the wall. Marisol jumped off the chair and ran to the front door.

Mercy's stepfather, Casimiro, walked in, his uniform soiled with car oil and engine grease.

Daddy, Marisol cheered.

I'm in the kitchen, Mercy shouted.

He walked into the kitchen and asked Mercy if she had seen her mother.

"I'm making food. You hungry? She pointed at

the eggs with the fork in her hand.

Casimiro didn't answer. He unzipped his navy blue jumpsuit and took off his grease-stained work boots. He pulled out a piece of gum and two lollipops wrapped in green cellophane.

"Here, Mija," he placed the candy on the glass kitchen table. The candy bounced and danced glass top.

"You have to eat first," Mercy said.

"Let her. I brought one for you too."

He reached into his other pocket, pulled out a cellophane tube stuffed with colored gumballs, and tossed them onto the table.

"Thanks, but we have to wait until after dinner, okay."

Mercy snatched the candy from the table and put it in the cabinet.

"Give it back," Marisol cried.

Casimiro's nostrils flared, just like Pershing. He stood up, standing over Mercy. "Give it back."

Mercy shook her head no. Before she could say anything, Casimiro slapped her across the face so hard that the smack shook the cabinet doors. The eggs sizzled and crackled violently.

"Give it to her, cabróna."

Marisol ran out of the kitchen, crying.

He raised his hand again and pumped it towards Mercy. She flinched, and he laughed. While he was laughing, Mercy gripped the fork tight in her hand.

"You're just like your mother."

He held his hand up. Mercy saw a solution in the fleshy part of his palm, a solution that would ensure her stepfather would never put his hands on her again. He pumped his hand to make her flinch. And Mercy played her part, acting real scared. She knew the threat and had learned to flinch and play real scared. An act that proved to Pepper that he had dominance over Mercy. It worked most of the time. This time she was ready. Instead of flinching, she gripped the fork in her hand and jammed it into the center of his hand. Blood squirted out of his hand and onto the frying eggs. Casimiro screamed and shrilled, gripping his hand. She had dug that fork in as deep as she could. Then she twisted the fork and heard something snap. Maybe a bone or a tendon? She could only be so lucky. She wanted to drive the fork into his heart and watch him bleed.

Casimiro pulled his hand away, then bent over to pull the fork out. He sent a tornado of cuss words in Mercy's direction.

She ran out of the kitchen, past her sister, crying in the hallway. She flew past the wrought-iron door and into the street. Her mother, Mary, was pulling up into the driveway.

"Stop!" Mary shouted. "Where are you going?"

But Mercy didn't stop. She kept running down the street until her pumping legs gave out, and she spilled over the asphalt, scraping her elbow and knees. When Mercy saw her mother's Oldsmobile turning the corner, she picked herself up from the floor and hobbled to the closest house. Mercy knocked on the door. No answer. The Oldsmobile pulled up the driveway, and Casimiro and Mary jumped out of the car. He had toilet paper wrapped around his bloody hand. Mother and her Stepfather were foaming at the mouth. Bombarding Mercy with insults.

"Get your ass over here, Cabróna," Mary shouted.

Casimiro held up his hand to show Mary the wound she had caused. The toilet paper was pink and wet.

Mercy flipped them the bird, then ran to the side of the house and jumped the fence where a little chihuahua dog barked and growled at her. The dog's thighs flexed, and its teeth gnashed at Mercy.

"Get over here, pinche Hija de puta," Mary yelled from the parked car.

The Chihuahua snapped at Mercy. She jumped back and reared her leg, punting the Chihuahua's head like a kickball, sending the dog a couple of feet back. It whimpered and whined, but she had no time to see if it was alright. She jumped the rock wall at the back of the yard. Her right ankle buckled as she landed. The Oldsmobile's engine turned over, and she could hear it circle around the street. It sounded like a train heading straight for her. She scanned the street and spotted a silver trash-can gleaming in the sun. She limped toward it as fast as her hurt ankle would allow. She climbed into the hot stinking trash can.

Mercy sat in the trashcan, baking in the smell of spoiled food. She heard the Oldsmobile drive by, her mother still shouting obscenities from the car window. The Oldsmobile circled back a couple of times before driving away.

"Don't come home, you puta," her mom shouted as she drove off.

A car pulled up onto the driveway. She peeked from the lip of the trashcan, expecting that Casi would be charging toward her. Instead, it was a Mrs. Witmore's teal van. Mrs. Witmore opened the van doors and pulled two little girls from the backseat. Mercy crawled out of the trashcan, and one of the girls screamed.

"Please, help me," an overheated Mercy whimpered.

Both girls screamed as Mercy crawled out and limped towards them. The girls hid behind their mother's rump.

"Are you okay?" Mrs. Witmore asked. You can stay here if you need. But I will have to inform your mother that you are here.

"Don't bother, Mercy said. "She's the one that put me here."

"I know," Mrs. Witmore said. "But I have to inform her anyway. It's the right thing to do."

No. Let me call a friend, please.

Mrs. Witmore agreed and walked Mercy into her house. Mrs. Witmore's house was clean. The carpets were not stained, and the walls were white and grease-free.

At first, Mercy called Lupita, no answer. She hesitated to call Santana, but maybe Lupita was with him, and things wouldn't get awkward.

"Hey, man," Mercy said over the phone. "I know this is like out of the blue, but you think you could scoop me up? I got nowhere to go. My stepfather is being a real shit-head, you know. I'll meet you at the usual spot."

Mercy handed the phone back to Mrs. Witmore. Mrs. Witmore had her address book out and started to dial Mary's number, but Mercy had run out the door before the rotary could stop spinning.

Mercy sat under the tree and watched a group of kids climb up a slide and go down it head first, then laugh all the way down. As Mercy drifted to sleep, Santana's avocado-green Chevette pulled up to the park. He honked his horn twice and opened the passenger's door. The noise was loud and crass, like he was honking for her to hurry up. The honking woke Mercy, and the sharp pain in her ankle shot up her leg. She hobbled over to Santana's car and got in. He leaned over and gave her a hug.

"You all right, girl?" He spoke in a low tone like he wanted to sound sexy.

"I really don't want to talk about it. Let's find Lupita and come back to the park."

"Loops went home," Santana said. "They're taking some lame-ass portraits or something. She said she'd call after."

"Let's stay here then," Mercy said. "Hang at the park, tu saves."

"I left my grass at home. Besides, no one's there yet." He put the Chevette in gear and pulled out. "You can clean up there. Cus' girl, you smell rank."

She watched as trees, stop signs, cacti, and houses blurred by. She did not want to be in this position. She liked Santana, but she loved her friend even more. She caught Santana's dark skin, greasy ponytail, chapped lips, and wispy mustache in the reflection on the passenger side window. He put his slender hand on her thigh, near her knee. She pulled it away.

"Don't worry, baby girl," Santana said. "I got you."

I don't want this, Mercy said.

He pulled his hand away and stayed quiet till they pulled up to his family's red-brick house.

"My mom won't be home till seven," he said. "You can shower or wash up in the bathroom."

Mercy had never been in Santana's room. She hesitated and then walked in. A giant flag of Mexico hung over his bed. El Ché, Hendrix, Santana, and Malo posters littered his walls.

This one's my favorite, Santana said. He pointed to a black and white poster of John F. Kennedy leaning over and saying something to Cesar Chavez while Chavez looks down at a row of crates filled with grapes. *Do you live in Camelot?* written in bold white letters at the bottom of the poster.

"Just goes to show you," Santana said. "Presidents don't know shit."

He motioned towards the bathroom with his hands. You can clean up in there. He handed Mercy a pair of sweats and an old Crosby Stills and Nash t-shirt.

The shower was warm, and she felt better. Her ankle had swollen, but either she got used to the pain, or the pain had dulled. After the shower, she dried her hair and returned to Santana's room.

"Take a seat," Santana motioned to the bed.

"I'm okay," Mercy said.

She walked around his room, eying his posters and books. She went over to a trophy on his desk. The plaque read first place, two hundred meters, Steve Garcia.

"Your real name is Steve?" Mercy laughed.

"Yeah, can you believe that shit? Dumb ass parents. But I convinced everybody to call me Santana instead. Pretty cool, Huh?"

He pulled a wooden box from his dresser drawer and handed it to Mercy. A swastika was carved onto the lid.

It used to be my brother's, said Santana. He gave it to me before he left for the Army. There are rolling papers and some Nag Champa in there.

He closed the door.

"Wait," Mercy said.

"I got to close the door, or my mom will be pissed if she smells pot in the house."

"Don't try nothing," Cabrón.

"Girl, be cool," Santana laughed.

He closed the door. Two posters were on the inside of his door. The top poster is Farrah Fawcett in a copper bathing suit. Beneath Farra's poster was a poster of a Tibetan monk meditating, despite being on fire.

Santana's mom barged in and caught them. Neither of them had heard her come into the house. Santana pulled jumped off of Mercy and pulled his pants up. Mercy pulled the borrowed Crosby Stills and Nash down over her torso. She was crying, but Santana's mom assured herself that Mercy was just embarrassed.

"I'm calling your mom," Mrs. Garcia said.

But before Mrs. Garcia could finish dialing, Mercy had blown past her and into the dark of the night.

In The Palm of the Gods

As I enter my grandmother's house, I call out her name. No answer. My stomach knots up. I know I'm about to find her sprawled out on the linoleum floor like she found my grandfather. I go to her room and find her asleep in her bed. Her mouth hangs open, and I can see her leathery gums. Her tender snores fade in the breeze of a fan by her bed. I tap her leg, and she snorts. Her body tenses, and she looks up at me, confused.

"Sharlie, what are you doing here?" she asks.

I haven't seen or called her in months, maybe more.

"Where are your dientes?" I ask.

"No se," she says. "I haven't seen them in a while."

I help her sit up. She stabilizes herself. I bring her a glass of water.

"Why are you here?" She asks again.

"To see you, Ma."

"Since when do you care about me?"

I reach into my back pocket and pull out a folded bank statement. I weaseled out of Margie. I took my time unfolding the paper because it took me weeks to convince her that my uncle was cheating.

"It took me a while to get this," I say. "It's a bank

statement showing the cashed check.

Monse puts on her reading glasses. The lenses magnify her eyes, giving her a look of excitement. She looks at the statement before tearing it into small pieces that she drops on the floor.

"What do I care about this?" she says.

"I just want to know why you lied for Jesus."

She steps into her slippers. "I'll make some food," she says.

I follow her into the kitchen. I need her to explain to me why they have lied to me. She pulls out a pan, lard, eggs, flour tortillas, and chorizo. The chorizo sizzles in the pan, and the flour tortilla swells and puffs with steam. She hands me a plate of burritos and shuffles off to her room. I leave the plate on the table and follow her.

"Go eat," she says.

"Why did you lie to me?"

"Can't you just leave me alone and let me die?" she says. "It's all I want."

"You're always going on about dying," I say. "Get over it. Pepper died, not you."

"Tienes razon," she says.

"Quit trying to martyr yourself. You're no saint."

"Santa, no soy," she says.

She pulls the sheets from her bed and then opens her drawers.

"Que buscas?" I ask.

"My teeth, I've been looking for those pinche dientes for weeks."

She gnashes her gums at me and looks through the drawer.

"I can't take this shit anymore," I say. "If you aren't going to talk to me, I'm leaving." I walk out of the bedroom, but she calls me back.

"I told you," I say. "I'm done with this. My voice grows hoarse and loud. I'm done with you and Jesus."

"You're going to leave me? Just like your puta mom left you?"

I shiver, my hands tremble, and my gut contracts.

"Let me tell you a little story," she says. "Your mom came to me one day, asking for money. She held you in her arms. You were skinny and dark, and your diapers reeked of shit. Your mother begged and begged. She needed a little money to hold her over and buy you some diapers. But I knew that if I gave her money, she'd come back as soon as she ran out. I couldn't have Pepper's bastard daughter stopping by. So, I offered to buy you. $527 with the condition that she'd never return. She sold you like a fucking donkey at a cattle auction. She never came back, not even a phone call, nothing. She's probably dead."

I want to slap the shit out of my grandmother. "Lies!" I say.

"What are you going to do?" she says. "Hit me like your grandfather did? Look how that worked out." She smolders like a hot comal.

"What are you talking about, loca?" I ask her.

"I heard your grandfather dying in the restroom," she says. He called out to me when he got home from his morning walk. I ignored him. I heard him vomit. And the cold smack of his body hitting the floor. When I opened the restroom door, I saw him spilled out across the floor."

"Call the ambulance," he said.

"But I closed the door and leaned my weight against it. I heard Pepper's last breath. He gurgled, calling out my name, Monse, Monse, Monse, then he died. I waited for a couple of hours before I called the ambulance."

"I'm done with you," I say.

"Don't act like he was all inocente," she says. "That pedaso de mierda beat the shit out of me any chance he got. Jesus got it worse, sometimes. But you, oh, no, not his Sharlie. By the time you came along, he'd stopped drinking. You were his little buddy. But don't think he stopped drinking because of you, por favor. It took Pepper killing Marqito. Then the marrano stopped his drinking. He ruined me and then killed my cousin."

I take a deep breath and try to move. My legs are mortared to the floor.

"Pepper spread his seed all over El Paso, too. He fucked anyone and anything. He left four kids back in Aldáma, a few in Juárez, and maybe one or two in Chihuahua. But he never left Jesus or me."

"Stop," I say. "I don't want to hear this shit anymore."

"I wish he'd left me," she says. "But he kept me around because I could take a sock in the jaw."

The tears pool and run down my face. I still can't move. My grandmother has me in a trance.

"Don't cry, maricón," she says.

She lies back on the bed and grabs my hand. Her hands are warm and crusty, like bolio bread. She puts a pillow over her face.

"Estoy gastada," she says from under the pillow. "I just want it to be done."

She pulls my hands over the cool cotton pillow.

"Don't be a maricas," she says. "Help me end this."

I try to let go of the pillow, but she digs her nails into my hands. She screams from under the pillow. "Come on, you worthless piece of shit. I don't want to live anymore. I need to be with my Viejo."

I'm trying my hardest to pull away.

"Be strong, Sharlie. For the first time in your life, be a man. Your mother left you because she knew you were weak. Sold you like nothing, like a piece of meat. She didn't want you, and neither did I."

I want to end this situation; I want to end her. She needs to stop talking. She needs to stop existing. I remember being a little kid holding Monse tight as she tells me a story. I think back to her standing in the rain, waiting for me to get out of school. A large smile on her face. Rain soaking her blouse, her umbrella swaying in the wind. I don't want her to die. I can't let her die. Dear God, help!

I try pulling away, but she has a mean grip on my hands, pulling them down to ensure I don't let the pillow go. I look around, frantic, to find anything to help me out of this situation. I look over the room until I notice a plaster bust of Jesus Christ's upper half on her dresser. His hands are cupped like he's receiving communion as his eyes look up to the heavens. This is God's son. Salvation. A crumpled-up napkin is nestled between the plaster palms of the bust of Christ. Monse's pink plastic dentures stick out from underneath the napkin.

I pull hard. But she's screaming at me to keep going, to hold her down. I start pulling away, and she's digging her nails into me hard. She can't hold on. I pull away, and the tops of my hands are bleeding from her nails.

"Sharlie!" She screams.

I take the dentures from Christ's palms and shake

off the dust. She sits up. Her face is red and sweaty. She reaches for the dentures and takes hold of them, working them into her mouth. Snot and tears run down her face. Her remaining yellow teeth grip the optic white dentures. She cries for a moment looking up at me. I can feel the heat radiating from my head. My breathing is erratic, and the tears are running down my face. My hands tremble. She reaches up and grabs hold of my arm. She pulls me down to the bed and hugs me like I'm her son. A son of mercy.

About the Author

About the Author

Carlos Fidel Espinoza writers amidst the vibrant energy of the US/Mexico border. His debut poetry collection, *How to Lie to a Customs Agent*, earned him the prestigious Southwest Book Award. Carlos's work has been featured on Vice, NPR, Words on A Wire, State of the Arts, the Border Tuner, and The Smithsonian Museum of the American Latino.

Step into his world, where words unravel the resilience and yearning of the borderland soul.

www.ingramcontent.com/pod-product-compliance
Lightning Source LLC
Chambersburg PA
CBHW011556190726
48287CB00010B/2925

* 9 7 8 1 9 5 3 4 4 7 5 0 0 *